About the Author

'I am myself a Norfolk man and glory in being so'(Admiral Lord Nelson – from the balcony of the Wrestler's Inn, Great Yarmouth, to the townspeople, 6th November 1800).

Chris Brett was born in Great Yarmouth, with its many connections to Nelson and the sea. After a grammar school education, Chris post-graduated and embarked on a successful career in town planning, in both the public and private sectors.

In 2005, the bi-centenary year of the Battle of Trafalgar, Chris joined the Nelson Society to pursue his lifelong interest in his Norfolk hero. In recent years he has served as Vice Chairman and Chairman of the Society and has written a number of articles about Nelson and related subjects.

Cover Design by Jason Hopper at District-6.com '

Nelson and the Slave Trade

A CIP catalogue record for this book is available from the British Library
ISBN: 978-1-7395264-0-5

Picture credits: Figures 1, 2, 3, and 10 copyright Chris Brett. Figures 4, 5, 6, 12, 13, and 14 all in the public domain. Figures 7, 8, 9, 11 copyright Alamy Images. Every effort has been made to establish the copyright of images. Should there be a need, any omissions will be corrected in future editions or reprints. Other copyright as asserted.

Admiral Lord Nelson

3. Transcript of the forged letter (NMRN version) 133
4. Cobbett's Political Register version 135
5. The Campbell Forgery 136
6. Transcript of the Campbell Forgery 138
7. The Clarke and McArthur version 140
8. The Nicolas version 141
9. The Laughton 'Naval Miscellany' version 142
10. Timeline 144
11. Letter to Lord Nelson from Simon Taylor, October 1802 146
12. A note on Nelson's handwriting 148
13. Nelson's letter to John Herbert, February 1790 151
14. Transcript of letter from Nelson to John Herbert, February 1790 154

End Notes **155**
Select Bibliography and Note on Sources **163**
Acknowledgements **167**
Index **168**

PREFACE

Horatio Nelson holds an almost unique position in British history. We have had many warriors, on land and sea, but none have been remembered so reverently as this son of an obscure country parson who became the finest leader of fighting men this country has ever seen.

He won his fame, of course, in tremendously dangerous times, when Europe was being torn apart and remodelled by two decades of savage warfare. Revolutionary and post-revolutionary France was the vortex of this huge and ultimately world-wide conflict. Throughout Nelson's lifetime France and Britain had been rivals for influence and empire. More than half of the reign of George III was spent fighting the French. Our islands, however, seem to have been ruefully inadequate to the contest in many respects. In those days military strength was typically based upon the size of its armies, which in turn required manpower. Yet in 1800 France had three times the population of Britain. The number of British regular soldiers peaked about 1813, when they topped a quarter of a million men worldwide. But the year before Napoleon Bonaparte had lost some half a million men in his Russian campaign alone, and still had the resources to recruit another army of similar proportions immediately afterwards. Few rational minds could then doubt that had Napoleon – a ruthless, ambitious and brilliant opportunist as well as the ultimate master of land warfare - invaded Britain the result would have been foregone.

But, of course, Britain was a collection of islands, and her fleet for the most part commanded the seas, generally unequalled in its size and efficiency. It was those wooden walls, backed by Britain's growing industrial might, which protected these islands from defeat. And no one wielded those resources more brilliantly than Nelson. To most Britons, therefore, Nelson was both a guardian and a deliverer. He stood defiantly between us and our enemies. A man whose health and well-being were destroyed by war – he lost an eye in Corsica, an arm at Tenerife, a scarring head wound in Egypt and, of course, his life off Cape Trafalgar – he epitomized the warrior who placed himself in harm's way for his country and paid the price, repeatedly. This helps us to understand the almost unprecedented public grief when the news of Trafalgar came home. The most remarkable naval victory in British history hardly seemed worth the death of Nelson. In the lavish state funeral and in the numerous memorials raised in the admiral's honour, many funded by public subscriptions from all classes of people, the nation attempted to articulate both its grief and gratitude for his life and sacrifice. It was their way of acknowledging a huge debt, just as today we annually salute the fallen of two terrible twentieth-century conflicts.

But now we live in different times, and ask different questions. Sometimes we make few allowances for predecessors who lived in bygone ages and whose imperatives, situations, morals and values were very different than our own, but we expect them to divine and understand ours. Despite the thousands of letters that Nelson left, however, he is not always easy to interpret. Much, of course, is paramount, such as his patriotism and sense of duty, but about so many issues of his time he said almost nothing. He was, of course, brought up in the quiet world of agrarian Norfolk, and went to sea at the age of twelve. Most of his life was spent afloat in the service of his country. And some of his responsibilities were mind-blowing. As commander-in-chief of the Mediterranean in 1803, for example, he had to control more than a million square miles of sea – an area three times the size of Napoleon's empire - with a handful of ships, dealing with half a dozen imperial powers of different persuasions and purposes, whilst maintaining his own forces at the end of a communication and supply line that stretched a thousand miles from England. Small wonder, then, that Nelson's correspondence was overwhelmingly dominated by his immediate professional concerns, and his opinions on many issues of the day at home are unknown or estimable only through disparate and often oblique references.

We know enough of Nelson to agree with his close friend Sir William Hamilton that he was of a "liberal" inclination. His care and compassion for fellow officers and sailors endeared him to them, and he bestowed gifts upon the poor and supported orphanages and charities for disadvantaged young people. But there was much that was unpalatable about Georgian Britain that escaped Nelson's surviving correspondence. For many of the British people, whether handloom weavers, women and children toiling in mines and workshops, and subsistence farm labourers it was a period of unremitting hardship and uncertainty, a period that spawned the beginnings of the politicization of the working classes. Nelson's thoughts about such subjects are difficult to recover, and so it is with the crucially important subject of the Atlantic slave trade and the slave economy of the West Indies. In uncompromising and unforgiving circumstances, public figures are not always able to act as they would have wished, but Nelson was not a cruel man by nature and tended to sympathize with the unjustly afflicted. Personally, I cannot believe that he would have condoned the gross inhumanity of the slave trade, although I think it possible that he might have had reservations about how abolition might best be achieved given the turbulence of the times.

And now we have this timely contribution by Chris Brett, a diligent researcher with a respect for historical accuracy. Plumbing for us the admiral's correspondence and actions, he has pulled together what is known of Nelson's views on slavery, race and colour, from his early collaboration with Native American auxiliaries to occasional dealings with people of colour, including the black revolutionaries of Haiti. Some of this material is new to me, and much of it is reproduced in full for our convenience. While more information may one day come to hand, this small volume represents about all we know about its subject at the present time. A valuable addition to the libraries of Nelson scholars and buffs, it should be read by anyone interested in making a rational assessment of a subject rather too often befogged by passion and prejudice on all sides.

John Sugden

(Dr John Sugden is the author of the much acclaimed two volume biography of Nelson: 'A Dream of Glory' and 'The Sword of Albion').

A BRIEF CHRONOLOGY OF NELSON'S LIFE

1758 Born Burnham Thorpe, Norfolk, 29 September 1758, fourth child of eight surviving of original eleven. Four brothers: Maurice, William, Edmund and Suckling, and three sisters: Susannah, Ann, Catherine. Father, Edmund, a rural parson; mother Catherine née Suckling.

1767 Catherine, Nelson's mother dies.

1770 Nelson persuades his elder brother to write to their father Edmund for permission to join his uncle, Captain Maurice Suckling of the Royal Navy, who is preparing his ship for war with the Spanish. Entered into the book of the *Raisonnable* as a midshipman, aged 12.

1771 Joins the *Raisonnable* in the Medway. Transfers to the *Triumph* in March and, in July, aged 12, sails to the West Indies in a merchant ship, the *Mary Ann.*

1772-3 Returns from the West Indies. Nelson signs up for an expedition to the Arctic in the bomb vessel *Carcass,* its mission to find a route to the Pacific. On his return appointed midshipman to the *Seahorse* to the East Indies.

1775-6 Invalided from ship with malaria and returns home.

1777 Passes exam for Lieutenant. Appointed to *Lowestoffe*, arriving at Port Royal, Jamaica, in July.

1778 Uncle Maurice Suckling dies. Nelson appointed First Lieutenant in the *Bristol*. Given first command of the brig *Badger*.

1779 Promoted to Post Captain in command of the frigate *Hinchinbrook*. Spain allies with France against Britain.

1780 Disastrous campaign to Nicaragua in which Nelson shines. Appointed to the frigate *Janus*. Returns to Britain too ill to take command.

1781 Appointed to command frigate *Albemarle* and escorts convoy to the Baltic.

1782 Sails to Quebec, joins Lord Hood's squadron off New York. Meets Prince William Henry (Duke of Clarence, future King William IV) for the first time. Returns to the West Indies.

1783 Fails to take Grand Turk Islands. Returns to England in June. October, peace with France. Nelson goes to St Omer to learn French.

1784 Returns from France and is appointed to command of the frigate *Boreas*, sails for the West Indies. Arrives English Harbour, Antigua, in July.

1785 In May Nelson meets Mrs Frances Nisbet, widow, on Island of Nevis.

1786 November to March Nelson is aide-de-camp to Prince William Henry, later The Duke of Clarence and King William IV.

1787 Marries Frances Nisbet at Nevis. Prince William 'gives away' Frances. Nelson returns to England, paid off, and is on half pay.

1788 'On the beach' in Norfolk. Advises the Duke of Clarence of the plight of the rural poor.

1793 Re-employed by the Admiralty. Appointed to command of the *Agamemnon*, sails for the Mediterranean. July, off Toulon. September meets the Hamiltons for the first time. October engages French frigates.

1794 Involved with the campaign to secure Corsica as a base for the Mediterranean fleet, injures his right eye at Calvi.

1795 Captures the *Çalra* off Toulon. Jervis succeeds Hood as Commander-in-Chief, Mediterranean.

1796 Appointed Commodore and joins the *Captain*.

1797 Leaves the Mediterranean in March. Plays a decisive role in the Battle of Cape St Vincent against the Spanish. Promoted to Rear Admiral. Created a Knight of the Bath. Hoists flag in the *Theseus*. In July involved in boat actions off Cadiz and abortive attack on Santa Cruz, Tenerife, where he loses his right arm. Returns home to Bath.

1798 Hoists flag in March in the *Vanguard*, joins fleet off Cadiz under Earl St Vincent. In July, dispatched to pursue the French fleet in the Mediterranean. 1st August destroys the French fleet at Aboukir Bay, Egypt, at the Battle of the Nile. Created Baron of the Nile in November. In December rescues the Bourbons of Naples (King Ferdinand IV & Queen Maria Carolina), evacuating them to Sicily.

1799 Nelson remains in the Mediterranean. Created the Duke of Bronte and given Sicilian estate. Transfers flag to the *Foudroyant*. Nelson embroiled with the Hamiltons.

1800 Captures the *Genereux,* one of two ships that had escaped at the Battle of the Nile. July – November, returns home overland through Europe with the Hamiltons, arriving at Great Yarmouth. Meets Lady Nelson in London. In April defeats the Danish at Copenhagen, in the *Elephant*. In July takes command of the Squadron of Particular Service. Failed attack on Boulogne. Buys Merton Place, Wimbledon.
1801 Takes seat in the House of Lords, giving first speech in October.
1802 His father, Reverend Edmund Nelson, dies in Bath.
1803 Sir William Hamilton dies. War declared with France. Hoists flag in *Victory*.
1804 Blockades the French Mediterranean ports. Spain declares war on Britain.
1805 French elude the blockade and escape across the Atlantic to the Caribbean, Nelson gives chase. Nelson pens letter to Simon Taylor of Jamaica. August returns home. September re-joins *Victory*. 21st October, the Battle of Trafalgar in which the British fleet under Nelson destroys the combined fleet of French and Spanish. Nelson mortally wounded.
1806 January 9th, interred St Paul's Cathedral, London.

FOREWORD

In August 2017 I was enjoying a stroll in the sunshine along the seafront at Weymouth when my mobile rang. "Have you seen the article in today's *Guardian?"* my caller enquired. I hadn't. The article in question, of which more later, was entitled '*Toppling statues? Here's why Nelson's Column should be next'.*[1]I duly purchased the paper to read the first of several attacks upon Nelson's reputation.

Like many Nelson 'enthusiasts' I was taken aback by the allegations made in the article: that Nelson was a 'white supremacist', racist and pro-slavery. I have read numerous books on Nelson and none of them had ascribed these characteristics to him before and, in such a heavily congested market, it would be surprising if at least one of his biographers had not made such claims if they held an element of truth. The author of the article, the journalist Afua Hirsch, was heavily criticised in both the press and television for the attack on our national hero.

In December 2018 the issue arose again with the publication of Professor Christer Petley's article *'Lord Nelson and Slavery: Nelson's Dark Side'* in the BBC History Magazine.[2] That article raised the issue of a letter written by Nelson to Simon Taylor, a wealthy slave-owning planter in Jamaica, upon whom Professor Petley is a leading expert. The letter apparently supports the contention that Nelson was pro-slavery.

Much has been made of this letter which has been reproduced in a number of biographies, including those by Clarke and McArthur, Nicolas and Laughton.[3]However, closer examination of these and other published versions shows that they are not consistent and that there are differences between them. The original letter, which would confirm which, if any, of these printed versions was accurate, appears to have been lost or destroyed.

It was becoming clear that the issue of Nelson, race and slavery was not going to go away particularly when, in 2020, Nelson's Column appeared on a crowd-sourced map of statues and monuments that purportedly celebrate slavery and racism. That map is known as

'Topple the Racists' and is a 'Stop Trump Coalition' project that supports the Black Lives Matter movement and the topplers of the Edward Colston statue in Bristol. The justification for the inclusion of Nelson's Column on the map is the *Guardian* article of August 2017. The purpose of this book, therefore, is to ascertain whether or not there is any substance to those allegations.

Of course the Black Lives Matter and 'Topple the Racists' movements, together with others, highlight important injustices in our society, many of which are the legacies of the slave trade and slavery. The purpose of this study is not to denigrate or belittle their campaigns. Nor is the purpose of this study to underplay the extreme horrors, inhumanity, dehumanisation or immorality of the slave trade. Rather its aim is to ascertain the beliefs and actions of one man, Admiral Lord Nelson, in relation to the issues of race and the slave trade.

The allegations against Nelson sit uncomfortably with our general conception of his character: brave, heroic, humane, loved by his men and one prepared to give up his life in doing his duty for his country in the face of Napoleonic tyranny. There is, therefore, a risk in seeking the truth, which may not reinforce our pre-conceived ideas but, rather, undermine them.

I am conscious that, in undertaking this study, it is set in a current, ongoing and broad debate about the British Empire and its legacy. As Sanghera points out it is difficult to find any aspect of empire that is not subject to intense academic argument and, one might add, polarised political positioning.[4] Any study of empire (which is way beyond the scope of the current exercise) embraces a wide range of matters including racism, white supremacy and the slave trade. The assumption, which I have sought to avoid, is that everybody (in particular, in this case, Lord Nelson) associated with the British state in the period of empire and colonialism was, de facto, racist and a white supremacist, unless proven otherwise, albeit that was part of the context within which they operated.

I am aware that terminology here is important. I have generally used the terms 'slave trade' and 'slaves' as these are the terms that were usually used during the period under consideration, although their use is by no means intended to 'sanitise' the de-humanising activity of the sale and ownership of people. Further I have used the terms 'anti-abolitionists' and 'planters' to denote those who sought to perpetuate this activity and were responsible for, and oversaw, the enslavement of others.

In seeking to understand and test the veracity of the allegations made against Nelson it seemed sensible to try to collect all relevant information. In this respect the numerous letters written by Nelson, and the record of his deeds and words, are a significant source of information. This study seeks to find statements Nelson made on the subject of race and slavery, however oblique or tangential. This study must thus be regarded as part of 'live' research, as it is likely that other material documents and information will be uncovered, for example, in collections of letters of Nelson's correspondents. The letters uncovered thus far are not in themselves sufficient to prove the case decisively one way or another. It is necessary to understand the context within which they were written, both at the micro, personal level and in respect of what was happening in the country at that time.

This is not as straightforward as it seems. The situation is highly nuanced and complex – slave owners, for example, often had black mistresses, with whom they co-habited and had children by, and whom they cared for. So having close personal relationships with black and/or mixed race people is not necessarily an indicator of a non-racist belief. In addition, terms such as 'white supremacy' and 'racism' are relatively new and in the modern world are quite absolute in their meaning. So caution needs to be used in applying these terms.[5]

All this, of course, raises another crucial question – is it appropriate to judge historical figures by the mores and standards of the 21st century? Daniel Hannan considers it facile to judge historical figures by how closely their views resemble ours and, in Nelson's case, by an opinion, however obnoxious (if indeed he held it), which was incidental to his story.[6]

The allegations against Nelson are a relatively recent phenomenon and the over-riding principle must be that his accusers should bring forward evidence to support their position. So far such evidence seems to be lacking, with accusations being based on contention rather than established facts or analysis. This book therefore seeks to find and evaluate what evidence there is. Nelson has been recognised as a national hero for over two centuries now, having fought many battles on behalf of his country. This, then, is his final battle – that for his reputation.

This book falls into three parts. The first deals with the contentions that Nelson was a racist and white supremacist; the second examines the Nelson-Taylor letter in relation to the abolition of the slave trade; and the third considers the implications of these allegations on our perception of Nelson.

The Nelson story has been covered extensively in the numerous books written about him, some of which are identified in the 'Select Bibliography' at the end of this book. This book does not seek to repeat that story but focuses on the specific issues of Nelson, race and the slave trade, although I have included a short chronology of Nelson's life at the beginning of this book, to help the reader understand the events which helped shape his life.

PART ONE: DEFAMATION

"It is easy to distinguish those who argue from fact and those who argue from notions" cited by Arthur Koestler in 'The Sleepwalkers'.

1.

A REPUTATION CHALLENGED

Introduction

The Georgian era, generally accepted to be c1714-1830, was a period of tumultuous change and energy. Dynastic continuity was maintained by George I (1714-27) and his sons who also oversaw significant developments and changes in the arts, sciences, global exploration and social development. Abroad, revolutionary ideas fomented upheaval and wars followed. This was the Age of Enlightenment.

The arts saw the emergence of the Romantic poets such as Shelley, Keats and Byron with their highly evocative language and themes, and mirrors were held up to Georgian society by authors such as Jane Austen. The changing world of the Georgians was portrayed in the art of Constable, Reynolds and Turner[1], amongst others, with Handel, Bach, Mozart and Haydn[2] being amongst the popular musicians of the period.

The era saw the stirrings of the industrial revolution, fuelled in no small part by the needs of the Royal Navy, and with it the migration of people from rural areas to the towns and cities, as the industrial revolution took hold. Advances were made in the fields of philosophy and economics. It was also an age of exploration. Cook sailed to the far side of the world, alighting upon Australia and New Zealand, and Captain Bligh made his epic journey after seeking breadfruit in the islands of the Pacific Ocean. 1773 saw the Royal Navy's first Arctic expedition. The expedition's purpose was to find the North Pole and a north-east passage between the Atlantic and the Pacific. Two ships set off with the naval crews accompanied by scientists and their instruments and new machines, all redolent of the spirit of the age and the desire for knowledge. A young boy, Horatio Nelson, aged just 14, was engaged as a Midshipman on that expedition[3].

Increasingly during the eighteenth century the order of society and people's position in it was challenged by the evangelical movement, which questioned the established orthodoxies. Radical ideas were at large with, for example, Thomas Paine's *The Rights of Man*[4], drawing on revolutionary ideas from France and America and fanning the debate about the relationship between religion, the monarchy and the populace at large. In England radical thinkers and evangelists sought changes to the political structures, but the results were less dramatic than those achieved in France. Towards the end of the century, the momentum behind those questioning one of the foundations of the growing empire – the slave trade – was also gathering pace.

Nelson Accused

For the past two hundred years or so Admiral Lord Nelson has held an exalted position in British history and has been synonymous with the notions of courage, duty and sacrifice in the service of the country. In that regard his character and reputation are ingrained in the national image and psyche and he is, in short, regarded as the epitome of the heroic Englishman.

Recently, however, Nelson's heroic reputation has been under scrutiny particularly in the wake of a re-assessment of major historical figures prominent in or associated with the slave trade, arising from Britain's role in shaping the world order of the period. In Nelson's case this is a relatively recent phenomenon.

As previously noted, the first significant attack came in August 2017 with the *Guardian* article 'Toppling Statues? Here's why Nelson's Column should be next'[5] which accused Nelson of being a white supremacist and claimed that he' ..used his seat in the House of Lords and his position of huge influence to perpetuate the tyranny, serial rape and exploitation organised by West Indian planters, some of whom he counted amongst his closest friends.'

The article was accompanied by an image of Nelson's statue being pulled down from the top of Nelson's Column in Trafalgar Square. There are several elements to the accusations: Nelson's use of his position in the House of Lords; the use of his position of huge influence; his friendship with West Indian planters, all aimed at maintaining the system of slavery; and accusations of racism and white supremacy. These accusations have been accepted at face value and used in the current debate about Nelson's views. These charges are serious ones to be levelled against any person in any age and for this reason alone deserve close examination.

Nelson and the Lords

Nelson was created a peer, 'Baron Nelson of the Nile and of Burnham Thorpe', in November 1798, in recognition of his significant victory at the Battle of the Nile. Following his victory at the Battle of Copenhagen in 1801, Nelson was elevated to 'Viscount Nelson of the Nile and Burnham Thorpe', a position which enabled him to take a seat in the House of Lords. Although Nelson attended the House of Lords on a number of occasions (from October 1801 to April 1803) he only addressed the House six times, all of which occasions are matters of public record, and not once did he speak or opine upon slavery or the slave trade.

Nelson first attended the House of Lords on 29th October 1801 upon which occasion he addressed the House by seconding a motion of thanks to Admiral Saumarez for his successful action off Algeciras during the summer of that year. On 3rd November he again addressed the Lords but surprised them by belittling the strategic value of Malta, Minorca and the Cape of Good Hope. A week later he seconded a vote of thanks to Lord Keith for the successful landings at Aboukir Bay, and the next day spoke in support of the agreements reached with the Baltic powers which were a result of his own Baltic campaign. On 2nd November 1802 he seconded the address of thanks for the speech from the throne and was pleased to note that 'the preparations to maintain our dignity in peace are not to be neglected'. The peace Nelson was referring to was the Peace of Amiens, resulting from the treaty signed between Britain and France in May 1802, signalling an end to hostilities between the two nations who had been at war since 1793. Nelson's final appearance in the House of Lords was on 21st December 1802 when he commented on the Naval Commissioners' Bill in relation to prize money. [6]

Other commentators have noted that he was not a great orator and that he limited himself to speaking on matters about which he was knowledgeable. Even then he was not without criticism. On the debate about the ownership of Malta one member condemned him as naïve and wondered how Ministers could 'allow such a fool to speak'.[7] (Even Captain Hardy, a close friend and colleague, on reading in the papers that Nelson had spoken in the House, opined 'I am sorry for it and I am fully convinced that sailors should not talk too much').The evidence, therefore, clearly shows that Nelson did not use his seat in the Lords to perpetuate the horrors of the slave trade and slave ownership as alleged. Neither is there any evidence that Nelson used the influence of his title to advance a case for the slave trade or slavery either within or outside the formal setting of the Houses of Parliament.

Nelson's 'influence'

From 1797 until his death at Trafalgar in 1805 Nelson was increasingly famous, and his exploits known to an adoring public. This is potentially the period of his 'huge influence'. During that period Nelson focussed his attention almost obsessively on defeating the French and their allies (and, of course, his amorous relationship with Lady Hamilton). Nelson was only a brief visitor to the Caribbean during this period, when he was in pursuit of the French fleet under Admiral Villeneuve, trying to bring that fleet to battle in 1805. His time was spent largely in the Mediterranean and there is no evidence, written or otherwise, that he turned his mind specifically to the slave trade during that period. Consequently at no time during this period (or any other for that matter) could he reliably have been said to use his reputation or influence 'to perpetuate the tyranny, serial rape and exploitation organised by West Indian planters' as alleged.

It is perhaps ironic, therefore, that Nelson DID seek to use his 'huge influence', not to perpetuate tyranny as alleged, but to secure the freedom of slaves, for example off Palermo in 1799, and North Africa in the same year. Following a disastrous attack by the Neapolitans on the French in northern Italy, Nelson succeeded in evacuating the royal court of King Ferdinand and Queen Maria Carolina from Naples, the capital of the Kingdom of the Two Sicilies. Together with Sir William and Lady Emma Hamilton the party arrived in Palermo, Sicily, shortly followed by the Kelim Efendi,'a genial old scribe from the Sultan of Turkey's divan'(i.e. an emissary from the Sultan of Turkey, Selim III). Efendi presented Nelson with the famous diamond Chelengk in recognition of his victory at the Battle of the Nile. Nelson's stepson, Josiah Nisbet, was to accompany Kelim Efendi back to Constantinople in the ship *Bonne Citoyenne.* As they were being rowed across the bay to the ship, the Turkish entourage were hailed by Turkish slaves, all Ottoman subjects, who were being held in a Portuguese man-of-war. Kelim Efendi sent back an appeal to Nelson to intervene to secure their release. Nelson wrote to the Portuguese commander, the Marquis de Niza in the following terms:

"My Dear Marquis
You have some Turkish slaves on board. I beg, as a friend, as an English admiral – as a favour to me, as a favour to my Country – that you will give me the slaves. In doing this, you will oblige your faithful friend, Nelson"

The Marquis agreed to this request and the 24 Turkish slaves were released and entered into the muster book (the list of men serving on the ship) of the *Bonne Citoyenne.*[8]As such they would have been treated as free men, working for wages as any other seaman. Nelson could easily have taken the view that, as a British officer, he was diplomatically unable to intervene in this matter.

Subsequent events demonstrated that in other spheres Nelson's influence was truly limited. For example, despite strenuous efforts Nelson was unable to secure a victory medal, from the Admiralty, for those who fought at the Battle of Copenhagen in 1801, nor was he able to persuade the government to award Lady Emma Hamilton a pension as a reward for her efforts in supporting the fleet with supplies prior to the Battle of the Nile in 1799. He had no influence at all with the King, who frowned upon his adulterous relationship with

Lady Hamilton. Nelson's lack of influence in these areas led to a real antipathy to those in positions of power. Indeed, when setting up home with Emma Hamilton in Merton, at the end of 1803, Nelson's resentment came to the fore: 'None but real friends shall come to Merton ..... none of the great shall enter our peaceful abode. I hate them all'.

Given that there is no evidence that Nelson used his seat in the House of Lords or his position of questionable 'huge influence' to perpetuate the slave trade and its attendant horrors, indeed quite the reverse, it is perhaps a moot and irrelevant point as to whether he counted some West Indian planters amongst his close friends, a key argument in the accusation made in *The Guardian* article. However that contention is examined below. Nelson was on duty in the West Indies on several occasions, as follows.

Nelson and the West Indies

1771-72

Nelson joined the Navy, strongly supported by his uncle, Captain Maurice Suckling, in 1770, at the age of 12. He was assigned to HMS *Triumph* which was semi-permanently moored at Sheerness 'the business with Spain being accommodated'.[9] Here he would learn small boat work and run errands but would learn little of life on the high seas. Then, in July 1771, Nelson was 'sent in a West-India ship belonging to the House of Hibbert, Furrier, Horton with Mr John Rathbone, who had previously been in the Navy, on HMS *Dreadnought*, Captain Suckling'.[10] It appears that Captain Suckling, Nelson's benefactor, had found a way of giving the young Nelson an opportunity of gaining experience of life at sea, by entrusting this part of his education to his old friend and colleague John Rathbone. Suckling and Rathbone had served in the West Indies and Rathbone was now captain of a merchant ship, the *Mary Ann,* bound for Jamaica and other islands in the West Indies. Little is known of the merchantman *Mary Ann* although the firm of Hibbert, Furrier and Horton traded in slave-produced commodities, shipping them from the West Indies to London. During this voyage it is known that Nelson remained officially on the books of HMS *Triumph,* a subterfuge aimed at preserving his Royal Navy sea time. Given Nelson's age and rank it is highly unlikely that he had any great direct contact with planters or slaves on this voyage, although Nelson returned 'a practical seaman, with a horror of the Royal Navy'.[11]

1777-1780

Nelson's second visit to the West Indies began in May 1777, under Captain Locker, whom Nelson held in high regard, a full six years after his first voyage, and shortly after Nelson's commission as Lieutenant. Even here Captain Suckling's influence was felt – he recommended Nelson to the newly appointed Commander-in-Chief at Jamaica, Rear Admiral Sir Peter Parker, who promised to promote Nelson to Captain. On 1st January 1779 Nelson became Master and Commander of the *Badger* and later that year he was promoted to Post Captain. In June 1770 Nelson handed over the *Badger* to take command of Fort Charles in Port Royal, Kingston. Here Nelson would have resided in the officers' accommodation until he took command of the *Hinchinbrook* in September 1779.

There is no doubt that during this tour Nelson would have met with a number of the islanders, including those in the planter class. Indeed, his closest friend from this time in the West Indies was Hercules Ross. Ross was born in 1745 in Glasgow. In 1761 Ross travelled to Jamaica where he amassed a fortune as a trader and naval prize agent. He had a mixed race Jamaican slave mistress, whom he later freed, before returning to Scotland in 1782. Ross entered into correspondence with Wilberforce and gave evidence, in 1790, to the Select Committee of the House of Commons into the abolition of the slave trade and became a staunch abolitionist. He had a long and enduring friendship with Nelson, with whom he corresponded regularly and affectionately. He named his son Horatio and Nelson stood as the boy's godfather. Condemned by the planter class of his former acquaintance, it is unlikely that Ross would have developed such a close bond with anyone expressing support for the slave trade, which Ross saw as 'contrary … to the laws of God and nature …'

It is also suggested by Petley that Nelson met the prominent slaver, Simon Taylor, during this period, and was probably introduced to him by Captain Locker.[12] (Nelson's relationship with Taylor is explored in more detail in Part Two). Evidence is scant on the degree to which Nelson mixed with the planter class, the majority of records being concerned with his naval affairs, but the extent to which they can be called close friends is open to conjecture.

It is telling that, while Nelson was on this station in this period, he was engaged in the ill-fated attempt to capture the fort at San Juan on the Mosquito Coast of Nicaragua. Nelson fought alongside a force which included Native Americans, (Indians as they were then called) and free black fighters. Native Americans were often called upon by European powers in the Americas. For example, Native Americans fought alongside the Canadians and French in seeking to repel Wolfe's campaign to capture Quebec in 1759. Not all officers understood their cultures and practices, often complaining of a lack of (European military style) discipline. Polson, the Nicaraguan expedition leader, sought that the blacks be treated with the utmost humanity, and, although the severity of his command led to complaints from the Native Americans they admitted themselves 'very fond of Captain Nelson'[13], who clearly valued them as brother warriors. This is generally indicative of the way that Nelson treated his fellow men, even at this early stage in his career.

During this expedition Nelson was struck down with a severe fever.

On his return to Port Royal he was cared for by a free black woman, Cuba Cornwallis, who gradually nursed him to a condition where he was able to travel back to England.

Nelson thus returned home to England in 1780. The San Juan campaign had lasted some five months, a substantial part of Nelson's posting.

1782-83

In August 1781 Nelson learnt that he had been promoted to the rank of captain of the frigate *Albemarle*. The American War of Independence was in full swing and Nelson was despatched to North America. In November he arrived in New York, via Quebec, where he met Lord Hood, who was gathering ships for a voyage to the West Indies, to head off an anticipated French attack on Jamaica or other British possessions. When Nelson met Hood on Hood's flagship, he also met Prince William Henry for the first time, who was a midshipman on board.

Nelson was keen to join Hood in the West Indies where he hoped for the opportunity of meeting the French in a major battle. Nelson got his way and followed his dream of glory. The West Indies station offered opportunities for prize money but Prince William Henry noted that Nelson was more concerned with distinguishing himself in battle than with money. In the West Indies the hoped-for battle did not materialise, although there were plenty of opportunities for prize taking and minor actions.

Much of this tour of duty was spent at sea although Nelson, no doubt, made shore excursions, not least to see his prize agent. In these shore visits he would have mixed with members of the ruling/administrative/trading classes. Indeed he wrote to William Locker in February 1783 noting 'many inquiries were made after you at Jamaica, by people of all ranks and colour'. The 'people of colour' would certainly have been free persons and not slaves.

Nelson's penultimate trip to the West Indies was in 1784.

1784-87

In 1784 Nelson arrived in the West Indies and in August of that year left Barbados for Antigua, the largest of the British Leeward Islands. In Antigua, English Harbour provided a safe and secure berth for the navy's ships especially during the hurricane season (August to October). Nelson spent the first few weeks of this tour of duty mainly confined to his ship, HMS *Boreas,* and largely unaware of the slave plantations on the island.

Nelson was nostalgic for Jamaica and regretted that he did not have a ship available to send provisions, which were in short supply in Port Royal, to Cuba Cornwallis.[14]Nelson's time in the Leeward Islands was particularly troubled. Although the Commander-in-Chief of the Leeward Islands, Rear Admiral Sir Richard Hughes, introduced

Nelson to all the prominent islanders, Nelson's view of them was not complimentary. He regarded them as 'disaffected and selfish'[15] John Sugden speculates that Nelson was referring, perhaps, to 'plantation managers who cheated their absentee landlords, drank the newly fashionable claret with mulatto mistresses, discarding any inconvenient offspring'[16] This is not a sympathetic view of slaveholders or their relationship with their slaves.

It was while on this station that Nelson ran into conflict with the islanders. Nelson, together with his good friends and colleagues the Collingwood brothers, William and Cuthbert, considered it their duty to enforce the Navigation Acts.[17] In summary the Acts sought that British merchandise, including that from the colonies, was carried in British ships thus maintaining the strong inter-relationship between naval power and trade, which in turn resulted in a thriving shipbuilding industry and ensured a supply of experienced seamen, some from the merchant class, which could be called upon in times of conflict.

Nelson and the Collingwoods sought to enforce the Navigation Acts without distinction and determined that the trade between the British West Indian colonies and the recently independent America, if reliant upon goods carried in American ships, was in breach of the Acts. The prevention of this trade put Nelson into direct conflict with the islanders, and with his immediate superiors and Governor Shirley of Antigua. In the event Nelson and the Collingwoods were supported in their approach by the Admiralty and the Government back home. Nelson's actions were aimed at supporting policies designed to protect British interests.

As a result the islanders excluded him from their social circles and instigated long running legal actions against him, some of which followed him back to England at the end of this tour of duty. Thus Nelson's relationship with slave-owning planters in the West Indies was difficult. He complained that he was persecuted by planters and other islanders from one island to another; so 'that I could not leave my ship'. He further noted in a letter to William Locker in 1758'.. I am not very popular with the people. They have never visited me, and

I have had not a foot in any house since I have been on the Station, and all for doing my duty by being true to the interests of Great Britain'.[18] The situation of Nelson's exclusion from the islands' society was only partially addressed by the arrival in the islands of Prince William Henry, whom Nelson was charged with 'chaperoning'. On Antigua, Nelson accompanied the Prince on a circuit of receptions and balls, where he was undoubtedly introduced to the island's elite, but which left him wishing for a return to active service at sea. He did eventually accept the hospitality offered by some islanders and as a result met Frances (Fanny) Nisbet, an islander widow, who was related to the planter class, and whom he eventually married on the island of Nevis in 1787. In March 1786 Nelson wrote to Fanny again expressing an awkward relationship with the islanders: 'The inhabitants here are heartily tired of my company. I am ready to give them my room; and they may assure themselves, I will not trouble them a moment longer than I can help; for although my person is with them, my heart, thoughts and affections are far off'.[19] He further expressed his disdain of the inhabitants of Antigua, where he was stationed, stating he would hold them 'very cheap in future; but I will have done with such trash'.[20]

Fig 1: Nelson's Dockyard, English Harbour, Antigua.

Fig 2: Copper and lumber store, Nelson's Dockyard.

Fanny's father, William, had been a senior judge on Nevis and a partner in the legal firm of Herbert, Morton and Woolward. He died aged 53 in 1779, before Fanny had reached the age of eighteen, her mother having died some years before. She married Josiah Nisbet, an Edinburgh qualified physician, after her father's death. Josiah Nisbet died in 1781, in England, where he and Fanny had set up home. After his death Fanny returned to Nevis where she cared for her uncle, a planter and slave owner on the island, Mr John Herbert, President of the Council of the Island of Nevis. Nelson supposed that Mr Herbert would provide well for his niece, but Herbert said that he could not do much for her during his lifetime, due to heavy expenses. It would fall to Nelson to provide for Fanny. Nelson approached his uncle, William Suckling, for financial help. One thing is clear: Nelson was not and would not be a beneficiary of the gains of slavery or the slave trade.
After their marriage Nelson and Fanny showed no desire to become part of the planter society and proceeded to Europe, where Nelson pursued his naval career with full vigour. (One commentator has even suggested that, despite her family background, Fanny thought the slave trade immoral).[21]

In November 1787 Nelson and Fanny arrived back in England after what had been, for Nelson, an exhausting and often difficult tour of duty in the Caribbean. They had little or nothing to do with the planter class thereafter, other than 'duty' visits to Fanny's relatives and friends in England. Nelson was never involved directly with the slave trade, never owned slaves or a slave plantation, never financed a slave ship, never took part in slaving activities at sea, nor did he benefit from marrying Fanny despite her relationship to the planter class in the West Indies. He never spoke in support of the slave trade nor had he any ongoing interest or involvement in the trade.

1805: The Final Visit

Nelson's final visit to the Caribbean was in pursuit of the French fleet in 1805. Napoleon had been gathering an army for the invasion of Britain but estimated that he needed three days free of the Royal Navy to complete the invasion. The French fleet, under Admiral Villeneuve, was to lure the British fleet away from the Channel by a feint to the West Indies. Nelson pursued the French fleet and reached Barbados on 4th June and, acting on intelligence, was led to believe that the French fleet was headed for Trinidad and Tobago. After picking up local troops, Nelson headed off to relieve those islands, only to find the intelligence had been false. Meanwhile, on hearing that Nelson was in pursuit, Villeneuve set sail for Europe. Nelson had little or no time, in this race to catch up with the French fleet, to mix with the islanders, although on 10th June Nelson penned the now infamous letter to Simon Taylor of Jamaica, a missive considered in detail in Part Two below. Nelson arrived off Antigua on 12thJune where it became clear he had just missed Villeneuve. Assuming that Villeneuve was heading back to Europe, Nelson again set off in pursuit, to ultimately meet his destiny at Trafalgar.

The route of Nelson's final visit is shown in Figure 3.

Throughout his career Nelson wrote several thousand letters, many of which survive today and which are reproduced in early publications such as *'The Life and Services of Admiral Lord Nelson'* by Clarke and McArthur, *'The Dispatches and Letters of Lord Nelson'* compiled by

Sir Nicholas Harris Nicolas and, more latterly, *'Nelson: The New Letters'* by Colin White (see select bibliography).

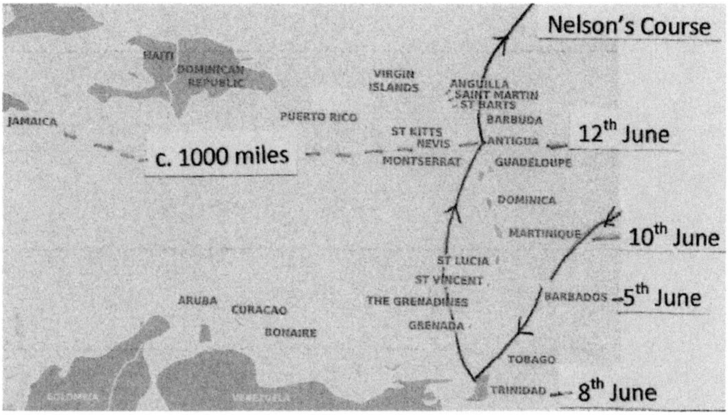

Fig 3: Nelson's Route in the Caribbean June 1805.

It is difficult to find any substantial references to race or slavery within these letters, which is hardly consistent with the actions or beliefs of someone who is purposefully and intentionally racist or a white supremacist. *The Guardian* journalist, Afua Hirsch, does not appear to have made clear the basis of her claims and in her subsequent book 'Brit(ish)' there is no reference to Nelson, although there is a reference to sculptures at the base of Nelson's Column in Trafalgar Square.

In the 18th and 19th centuries Britain was a colonial power, the wealth and operation of the colonial system being based, *inter alia*, on the slave trade and protected by the Royal Navy. As a commissioned officer of the Crown, Nelson was obliged to uphold the law, as set by Parliament. That was his duty. He consequently had no agency in respect of the slave trade or slavery. The central question, therefore, is: was it possible for Nelson, a serving naval officer, to support the colonial system, of which the West Indies were an integral part, without being pro-slavery or racist? Understanding the views of the Royal Navy will help assess Nelson's stance on these matters.

2

THE ROYAL NAVY

In the 18th and 19th centuries the British Isles and its colonies were conceived as one large and complex system although opinions differed about the importance of the sections of the empire and relations among them. There was, however, general agreement that the success of the empire and national security were inextricably linked. The role of the navy was central in delivering this concept of empire, the security of trade and defence of the nation. To that end the Governments of the day invested heavily in defence of the maritime Atlantic trade, establishing bases in the Caribbean such as at English Harbour in Antigua.[22]

A significant proportion of Britain's wealth was generated by the Caribbean islands' produce, particularly sugar, which in turn was underpinned by slavery. Britain's wealth was generated from a maritime system in which overseas trade paid for the navy whilst merchant shipping trained the seamen who manned it, thus enabling the navy to protect trade. The merchant marine became a valuable source of manpower particularly in times of conflict with foreign powers. A number of flag officers who gave evidence to the parliamentary inquiry into the slave trade in 1790 supported the slave trade as it performed that very function. Nelson, a captain who had relatively recent experience of serving in the Caribbean, and who was well known at the Admiralty due to his stance on the Navigation Acts, was not called upon to give evidence to the inquiry.

Whilst legislators accepted the morality of abolition of the slave trade, they sought assurances that it would not undermine economic and maritime security. Henry Dundas, the Home Secretary, for example, argued that to maintain an extensive and complicated war it was necessary to destroy enemy colonies whilst adding to British maritime strength – naval might and the colonies were seen as being inextricably linked.[23]

Both the Prime Minister, Pitt the Younger (Prime Minister 1783-1801,1804-1806), and the champion of abolition of the slave trade,

William Wilberforce, accepted that the Caribbean sugar plantations were of fundamental importance to the nation and that British interests needed to be reconciled with the abolition of the slave trade, requiring an improvement of the colonial system.[24] At the time, therefore, it seems that politicians were able to 'de-couple' the colonial system from the slave trade and slavery, and there is no reason to think that Nelson could not do likewise. The pro-slavery lobby sought to close this distinction arguing that the wealth of the colonies, and hence Britain's prosperity, was inextricably linked to slavery (and hence the slave trade), an argument with which they persisted throughout the period to the abolition of slavery itself. This argument was one of many employed by the pro-slavery lobby in an attempt to undermine the abolitionist movement.

A number of ideas for reform of the system were suggested, such as those of Lt Layman RN, whose proposals are considered in Part Two[25]. Indeed, initially, even Wilberforce did not propose the emancipation of slaves outright. Rather he argued that the abolition of the slave trade would, in consequence, improve the conditions of existing slaves – even in the wake of the decision to abolish the slave trade in 1807 Wilberforce made it clear, at that time, that total emancipation was not the immediate goal.[26]

Nelson, of course, was a beneficiary of the system of marine shipping providing trained seamen for the navy. His first major seaborne voyage, at the age of thirteen, was to the Caribbean on a merchantman. In his autobiography, written in 1799, Nelson said of this voyage that he 'came back a practical seaman'.[27] However, nowhere in his autobiography did Nelson suggest that his experience (training) was a benefit of the slave trade, as several flag officers had done a few years before in their evidence to the parliamentary inquiry into the slave trade. Rather Nelson saw it as part of the evolution of his naval career, although he recognised a dislocation between the merchant service and the Royal Navy returning, as he did, with 'a horror of the Royal Navy'.

The manning of the navy was a constant issue and the problem of finding and recruiting men was a serious concern in times of war. Volunteers were the basic raw material for manning the navy, supplemented by impressed men. In addition to the impressed men, another minority which fulfilled an important role in manning the navy was black seamen, both slaves and free men. The navy's attitude towards the slaves was generally liberal when compared to the slave societies from which they had come. The Admiralty was inclined to regard a man-of-war as a little piece of British territory in which slavery was improper. Slaves fleeing enemy plantations were also accorded the same consideration and protection as any other man on board, as were seamen impressed into the service.[28] For example, in the case of Castillo, a slave seaman who absconded from his master in 1758, having spent five years serving on a merchantman, and then on board a navy vessel, the Admiralty responded robustly to his request for protection. Having recaptured him, his master threatened to sell him in Barbados. The Admiralty made it clear that it had no objection to a seaman being pressed into the service but, once in, he was entitled to the same protection and consideration as any other seaman.[29] Such attitudes would have been prevalent during Nelson's period of service. That black sailors were a feature of the Georgian navy is borne out in paintings and art forms of the period. The presence of black sailors in these images such as in Dighton's 'Death of Nelson'(*Figure 5*) and on the relief at the base of Nelson's Column, was not due to any form of political correctness but, rather, that they were a reasonable representation of the reality on board ship. Those sailors are shown undertaking a range of duties and activities alongside their white counterparts, and taking part and suffering in the Navy's battles. It is also evident that a number of black sailors were accommodated and looked after at the naval hospital in Greenwich, from the mid 18th century onwards.

This 'protective' attitude of the Royal Navy sometimes extended beyond the navy's ships. Recent work undertaken by Christopher Waters and Desley Gardner at the naval dockyard in Antigua has found evidence of Antigua's first modern black settlement. The dockyard relied on enslaved Africans, 'The King's Negroes', to help fulfil its functions. These men formed the basis of an African community outside the dockyard walls in an area known as the Middle Ground. This settlement was distant from the plantations on the island and allowed for the creation of a community that was supplemented by runaway slaves, who were absorbed into the existing villages of the enslaved Africans serving the naval dockyard. This community existed in what Waters and Gardner describe as the 'liminal space between the colonial government and military establishment', on Royal Navy land but outside the confines of the dockyard, where jurisdictional responsibilities were blurred.

Fig 4 A gun crew at mess.

The Middle Ground, in effect, fell nominally under the Royal Navy's control and protection, and tensions between the civil government of the island and the military arose when it was clear that the navy was extending the same asylum to runaway slaves as those found on His Majesty's ships. The navy's unwillingness to accede to the demands of the civil government (for the repatriation of runaway slaves) and its

Fig 5 Detail from The Death of Nelson (Denis Dighton 1825).

recognition of the growing settlement at Middle Ground can be seen as expedient in terms of self-interest – simply put: the dockyard could not fulfil its functions without the engagement of the enslaved Africans, albeit that they were treated as other enlisted men.[30]

Costello estimates that towards the end of the period of the British slave trade some 3 per cent of all crewmen were black mariners, but it is likely that the numbers trading directly with the West Indies were far larger.[31] Black sailors, including slaves, continued to be recruited into the navy, especially in times of war, enabled by an amendment to the Navigation Acts. This amendment included slaves resident in the West Indies in the definition of being 'British'. Once employed they were subject to the benefits afforded to other sailors.

Against this background it is inconceivable that Nelson would not have served alongside black sailors. He would have undoubtedly come across black sailors on his first trip to the West Indies in the *Mary Ann* and from that time forward would have served alongside them throughout his career. It is also highly likely that he met Olaudah Equiano, also known as Gustavo Vassa or Gustav Feston, a former slave prominent in the movement to abolish the slave trade, who served as an Able Seaman on the HMS *Racehorse* in the Arctic expedition in 1773 (Nelson served on the accompanying ship HMS *Carcass* – see End Note 3).

Equiano was born and raised in southern Nigeria. As an 11-year-old child he was captured and enslaved, and over the years was slave to a number of seafaring owners. He learnt to read and write and eventually bought his own freedom. He became an ardent abolitionist and his memoirs *'The Interesting narrative of the Life of OLAUDAH EQUIANO or Gustavus Vassa, the African, Written by Himself'* were published in 1789. As a free man he entered the service of Dr Charles Irving whom he accompanied on the Arctic expedition. In 1777 he settled in England and became increasingly involved in the Church and the abolition of the slave trade movement. In his memoirs Equiano records that, as a free man, he signed on to both the Royal Navy and the merchant service. He married an Englishwoman, Susannah Cullen, in 1792. Equiano died in 1797, a year after Susannah.

Fig 6: Olaudah Equiano

There were a number of black sailors on board HMS *Victory* at Trafalgar.[32] The relatively egalitarian approach to black sailors on board ship can be contrasted to the relationship that persisted between slave owners and slaves on the plantations with its attendant horrors and subjugation, regardless of any intimate relationships that may have existed between slaves and their masters. It is not surprising that Nelson had little to say on the racial background of his fellow sailors, all of whom he was to depend upon in conducting his naval campaigns.

The on-board approach of protection accorded by the navy towards its sailors, regardless of ethnicity, would seem entirely consistent with Nelson's world view in which meritocracy, humanity and compassion were component parts.

3

PERSONAL RELATIONSHIPS

Nelson was clearly in contact with peoples of various ethnicities. It is possible to glean some insight into his views on race in his dealings with particular individuals.

James Marguette

On 19th January 1805 the Mediterranean fleet, under Nelson, was moored in Agincourt Sound (in the Maddalena Islands at the northern end of Sardinia) when news arrived that the French fleet had left Toulon. Nelson had no intelligence as to where the French fleet was headed and he surmised, wrongly, that it had headed east to Alexandria. There was no sign of the French fleet at Alexandria and, on arriving in Sardinia, Nelson learned it had returned to Toulon, having been damaged by Mediterranean gales. Nelson posted a frigate picket line off Toulon but Villeneuve and the French fleet slipped out unseen, leaving Nelson able to 'neither eat, drink or sleep'.

On 19th April he received the news that Admiral Villeneuve had passed through the Straits of Gibraltar some 10 days earlier and that the French fleet was now in the Atlantic where it was accompanied by six Spanish ships under Admiral Gravina. On 10th May Nelson reached Lagos Bay, Portugal where he received firm intelligence that the combined fleet was heading for the Caribbean. Nelson set off in pursuit arriving at Barbados on 4th June. It was there that he picked up James Marguette ('a man of colour') who for many years had piloted British ships from Barbados to the different Leeward Islands.[33] Nelson's reasoning was that Marguette could pilot the fleet to any of the Leeward Islands in pursuit of the enemy.[34] Nelson took Marguette with him when he left Antigua on 13th June (just three days after he had penned his private letter to Simon Taylor) as he wanted a pilot acquainted with Porto Rico and Jamaica in the event that it was discovered that the enemy fleet had gone to either of those destinations.

It quickly became clear that the combined fleet was heading back to Europe and Nelson retained Marguette on board, there being no opportunity to return him to Barbados other than by a passage from England. Nelson finally arrived back in England in August 1805 but before leaving HMS *Victory* he wrote, on 18th August, a letter to William Marsden at the Admiralty seeking that Marguette be particularly taken care of, as follows[35]:

Victory, at Spithead, 18th August 1805

Sir,
I must beg you will good enough to recommend James Marquette (Pilot), the bearer hereof, mentioned in my letter in original and duplicate dated the 10th ult, to their Lordships' kind attention. He is a most valuable and useful man as a Pilot for the Leeward Islands, and very handsomely volunteered his services to me, as mentioned in my said letters; and as he is a perfect stranger in London, and consequently will be apt to be imposed upon, I must beg that he be taken particular care of, and put in a way for a speedy passage to Barbadoes. I have paid him, as per Certificate from the Captain of the Victory, at the rate of 5s per day , from the 14th of June to the date hereof, as he has no money to defray his expenses during his stay in England; and beg, if their Lordships consider him entitled to more, that they will be so good as to order him to be paid; and also furnish him with such a further sum as they may think proper, to defray his expenses, and be some compensation for the inconvenience and loss he may sustain in the absence from his home. I must also beg, when their Lordships order him a passage in any of His Majesty's Ships, that they will be pleased to direct him to be borne as a Pilot, that he may receive the allowance as such till he arrives at Barbadoes.
I am, Sir, &c
NELSON AND BRONTË

Marsden was an Irish orientalist, numismatist and linguist who was appointed to the post of Second Secretary to the Admiralty, later rising to First Secretary. (It was in that capacity that he received the news of the victory at the Battle of Trafalgar and of the death of Lord

Nelson). In the letter Nelson requests that Marguette be given a speedy passage to Barbados and that his expenses be defrayed during his stay in England, and that he be further rewarded for his services and any losses he might sustain in his absence from Barbados.

These letters clearly show Nelson at his most humane and empathetic best, and show his appreciation of persons regardless of their ethnicity. In a footnote to this story it is also clear that the admiration Nelson held for Marguette was reciprocated. On 14th September 1805 Nelson took his last walk on English soil. This event was witnessed by an American, Benjamin Silliman, a strong opponent of slavery, who recorded the scene in his journal.[36] Nelson's departure from Portsmouth is also vividly described in 'Nelson's Last Walk' by Colin White.[37] He describes how Nelson pressed his way through the gathered crowds, sorry that he did not have two arms so that he could shake hands with more friends. What is not recorded by Colin White or Benjamin Silliman is that Nelson specifically singled out James Marguette. This event was reported, for example, in *The Carlisle Journal* on 5th October 1805 thus:

'On the arrival of Lord Nelson at South Sea Beach, and previous to his getting into his ten-oared cutter to embark on board the Victory, he took a most affectionate leave of Admiral Coffin, and some other officers who had attended to witness his departure. On his inquiring for Mr Martin, a man of colour, who had piloted his Lordship during his late voyage through the West Indies, he very good naturedly told him to give his fist, and complimented him as being a very honest man, and begged his remembrance to all friends in the West Indies, and then bid the surrounding multitude adieu!'

There is no doubt that 'Mr Martin' was James Marguette, his name probably being misheard by the reporter (there was only ever one black pilot on HMS *Victory* during the pursuit of the combined fleet). That Marguette had taken the trouble to travel from London to see Nelson depart shows the mutual esteem between the two men. An article by J. D. Ellis, on the website 'Historycalroots.com', concludes 'It is perhaps an irony that the last handshake Nelson, a fierce defender of the plantocracy, had prior to leaving British shores for the last time, was with a black sailor'.[38] Notwithstanding that there is no evidence that Nelson was a defender of the plantocracy, fierce or otherwise, there was no irony in the action at all. Indeed it was a show of mutual respect and affection between two men who had served together. It should be noted that Ellis' article was published on 20th October 2020, before the Nelson-Taylor letter, referred to in the Foreword and which is considered in depth in Part 2 below, was revealed as having been subject to forgery. The forged letter is probably the source of Ellis' claim that Nelson was a fierce supporter of the plantocracy.

James Price

William Suckling was Nelson's uncle, brother to Nelson's mother, Catherine Suckling. In 1772 he was appointed Deputy Collector of Customs in London. Nelson, aged twelve, had visited him in London in the company of his father a year earlier. William's mansion was in Kentish Town and boasted ornamental grounds, and fine furniture.
Present in the household was a black butler named Price, whom Nelson had met on several visits to his Uncle William's house. Nelson's uncle, of whom he was very fond, passed away in 1799 and Nelson felt the loss keenly. On the death of William, James Price moved to serve Nelson's older brother, Maurice.
In 1801, upon the death of Maurice, Nelson wrote to Lady Emma Hamilton with whom he was seeking to set up home, stating:

'I am sure you will comfort poor blind Mrs Nelson. Whatever you do I will confirm: and there is an old black servant, James Price, as good a man as ever lived, he shall be taken care of, and have a corner in my house as long as he lives'.[39]

Nelson's comment about James Price is indicative of the esteem with which he held those who had given good service, regardless of their ethnicity. In the event Price declined the offer as 'poor blind Mrs Nelson', (in fact, Susannah Ford, Maurice's common-law wife), was left with adequate funds to maintain her independence and James

Price stayed in service with her. Upon her death in 1811 Price was the sole beneficiary of her will.

Cuba(h) Cornwallis

Cuba Cornwallis was originally a slave owned by Captain William Cornwallis, a close service friend of Nelson in the West Indies, whom Nelson first met in 1778. Cornwallis appointed Cuba as his housekeeper upon granting Cuba her freedom and she remained in Jamaica when he departed, setting up home in Port Royal.

Cuba was a nurse who became well known for her treatment of the sick, using home remedies. When Nelson returned from the Nicaraguan campaign in 1780, seriously ill and probably suffering from a combination of diseases including dysentery, William Cornwallis and Admiral Parker, Commander-in-Chief of the Royal Naval forces in Jamaica, entrusted Nelson's care to Cuba. After a week Nelson was sufficiently recovered to make the journey back to England, during which voyage he was personally attended to by William Cornwallis. Cuba had a well-respected reputation as a healer and included amongst her other patients was Prince William Henry, the future king William IV.

Nelson, perhaps for entirely understandable reasons, retained an affection for Cuba. In October 1784 he wrote to William Cornwallis from Antigua:

'... poor Jamaica what a sad calamity. I wish any vessel was going from this place that I might send something to poor Cuba, for provisions are in great plenty here, and I suppose very dear at Kingston'.[40]

The 'sad calamity' which had befallen Jamaica, and to which Nelson refers, is likely to be the havoc wreaked by successive hurricanes. The hurricane of July that year caused immense damage and loss of life and this was compounded by 'two severe shocks of earthquakes' *(The Gentleman's Magazine 1784; West India Advices)*. Buildings were destroyed and ships sunk and food supplies lost.

Cuba Cornwallis lived to a good age eventually dying in 1848, although her exact date of birth remains unknown.

Fatima Emma Charlotte Nelson Hamilton

Fatima was a maid or servant to Emma Hamilton. Fatima's origins are somewhat unclear. She was apparently Sudanese or 'Nubian' and was 'taken out of a slave ship' by Nelson[41] from a Sudanese dealer who came aboard Nelson's ship after his famous victory at the Battle of the Nile. Fatima was placed under Emma's protection[42] and was a member of the entourage that undertook the overland return in 1800.[43] Nelson had defied Admiralty orders to return immediately to England, to undertake a return to England overland across Europe. He was accompanied by the Hamiltons in a trip designed, in part, to exploit Nelson's celebrity and to give him more time to spend with Lady Hamilton.

Fatima was also to feature in dancing performances by Emma.[44] Fatima worked as a maid to Emma at the house in Merton, where Nelson and Emma had set up home, and possibly as a nursemaid to Nelson and Emma's daughter Horatia. Servants and maids in the Nelson/Emma household received half a guinea a month as well as board and lodgings. Fatima was christened as a 20-year-old on Emma's birthday, Fatima being the name of the patron saint of Naples. The day was somewhat overshadowed by news of Nelson's father's illness (his father died the next day). Nelson attended the baptism rather than visiting his father, for fear of upsetting his wife, Fanny, who had attended to Nelson's father during his illness, after Nelson and Fanny's separation.

In October 1801 Nelson wrote to Emma, after his early appearances in the House of Lords, stating that he would rather hear Emma tell of an:

'...anecdote of Fatima ... than any speech I shall hear in Parliament'.[45]

Fatima was clearly an important and well-loved member of the Nelson household. After Nelson's death at Trafalgar and Emma's subsequent decline into penury Fatima remained with Emma until her debts were too great to support any servants. Sadly Fatima was unable to find any subsequent employment and ended up in the Bear Lane workhouse where she suffered a breakdown and was sent to St Luke's lunatic asylum where it is believed she died in 1810.

Catherine Despard

Catherine Despard was the wife of Colonel Edward Despard, an Irishman, who was the last person in Britain to be sentenced to be hanged, drawn and quartered for treason, although the sentence was subsequently commuted to hanging and post mortem beheading. Edward Despard had been with Nelson in the San Juan expedition, whilst Despard was serving with the 50th Regiment, nearly a quarter of a century before. Despard was charged with treason in relation to a plot to seize the Bank of England, the Houses of Parliament and the Tower of London, and to assassinate the King. Nelson was subpoenaed to give evidence for the defence at Despard's trial. Under cross- examination Nelson confirmed that he had not seen Despard in twenty years but when he served with him '*no man could have shown more zealous attachment to his sovereign and his country than Colonel Despard did. I formed the highest opinion of him as a man and an officer'*.

In the event the evidence against Despard was overwhelming and he was found guilty. Nelson did seek a pension for Mrs Despard, who was '*violently in love'* with Despard. (Nelson did not expect the pension to be awarded due to Edward Despard's refusal of the prayers of the prison chaplain whilst on the scaffold). Catherine Despard was of African descent and was comforted by Lady Hamilton after the execution. Bulkely, a longstanding friend of Nelson's, who had also served with him at San Juan, forwarded a sum of money to be passed on to Mrs Despard and it is likely that Nelson added to this.

The warmth and affection with which Nelson spoke about and acted towards Cuba Cornwallis, James Marguette, James Price, Fatima and Catherine Despard shows that his relationship with his fellow men and women was driven by humanity and compassion. However as noted in the Foreword, having black acquaintances was not necessarily an indication of non-racist beliefs, although as far as recorded he never spoke disparagingly of persons of different ethnicities. A search of Nelson's correspondence may give a further insight into his views on race and slavery.

4

RACE AND SLAVERY: THE LETTERS

There are only a limited number of references to race and/or slavery in the many thousands of Nelson's letters which have survived. Those references are assessed here.

John Herbert

On February 28th 1790 Nelson wrote to John Herbert, Fanny's uncle, in Nevis. At the time Nelson had been stood down and was on half pay (otherwise known as being 'on the beach'). This letter does not appear to have been reproduced in any of the many volumes of Nelson's letters, printed after his death and only came to light late on in the course of writing this book. The letter is in the hands of a private collector and is reproduced here with his kind permission. This is the first time in many years, therefore, that this letter has been available for consideration. It contains, as far as can be established, the earliest reference Nelson makes to the slave trade. The letter deals with the House of Commons Committee on the slave trade as well as other, personal and military matters. The relevant part of the letter is as follows (original spelling retained):

'*My Dear Sir*

I was in London a few days ago in order to show myself to the Great World, when I call'd on Mr Frasier to make enquiries after you. I was glad to hear from him you where in very good health. The Slave Trade Committee of the House of Commons go on but very slowly nor I believe have the most sanguine advocates for abolition nor any thoughts beyond regulations. My firm opinion is nothing serious will be done - for if the House of Commons from electioneering motives should bring in any bill which may affect the interests of the West Indies, the Lords-nor King would ever allow it to pass. The West India Colonies are too valuable for this country to injure. Sugars rais'd one penny per pound. It will be higher owing to the very small quantity of sugar made at St Domingo by their becoming Patriots which has occasioned in the short time I was in Town 3000 hogshead being exported. We are now near Josiah who is just fell down with measles.....'

In this letter Nelson is reporting to a relative, who is a slave owner, that he believes that even the most optimistic abolitionists are not expecting an outcome other than the regulation of the slave trade. He voices the opinion that any outcome that would injure the West Indies would never be allowed to pass through the (House of) Lords and would be resisted by the King (George III). He is of the view that the colonies are too valuable to be harmed. This view was one also held by a number of abolitionists, including Wilberforce, who sought change to, rather than dismantling of, the colonial system. The letter is really a report on the state of play of the process of the House of Commons Committee and the opinion voiced by Nelson is merely a statement of his view on the likely outcome of that process. It reveals nothing of Nelson's personal thoughts on the slave trade – he does not, for example, even infer that his opinion of the likely outcome of the Committee would, in his view, be a good or desired outcome.
The original letter is reproduced in Appendix 13, and a full transcript of the letter can be found in Appendix 14.

William Locker

William Locker was particularly dear to Nelson. He was Nelson's first Captain and became his mentor and friend. It was he who first advised Nelson 'Lay a Frenchman close and you will beat him', a sentiment adopted by Nelson in the adage 'Engage the enemy more closely'.[46] Throughout his life Nelson corresponded regularly with Locker covering matters such as naval affairs, conflict with the French and personal matters. It is probable that Locker was a slave owner. In 1784, for example, Nelson wrote to Locker regretting he could not give Locker information about Locker's estate in Dominica. Located between Martinique and Guadaloupe, Dominica was, at the time, a slave island. Originally neutral and then falling under French control, the island was ceded to Britain after the Seven Years War in 1763, was subsequently recaptured by the French and finally re-ceded back to Britain by the Treaty of Paris in 1783. There is no further reference to Locker's estate or slave ownership in the numerous items of correspondence between Nelson and Locker.

On 4th March 1796 Nelson was on active service off the coast of Italy. He wrote to Locker setting out at some length his concerns about the French intentions in respect of Italy. He then commented:

'How unfortunate Admiral Christian has been. I hope our West India Islands will not suffer more than they have done; but I see Wilberforce is meddling again with the slave trade. I feel very much obliged by Simon Taylor's remembrances; pray do not forget me to him when you write ……'

Nelson then went on to say that there is no station he would like more in time of war than Jamaica, which he felt he could keep free of privateers, which is '*the general complaint against our Admirals'*.[47]

Admiral Christian had set sail from St Helen's, in November 1795, with a squadron of ships, a convoy and some 16,000 troops to act against the French and Dutch settlements in the West Indies. The fleet was dispersed by storms and after repairing their damages set sail again at the beginning of December when it was once again dispersed by gales. The fleet returned to Spithead.

In 1796 Wilberforce had succeeded in bringing forward a bill for the abolition of the slave trade (the 'meddling' to which Nelson refers) although this was rejected in the Commons by 74 votes to 70 on March 15th. In his letter Nelson is expressing his concern that the 'unfortunate' event relating to Admiral Christian had left the West Indian Islands vulnerable, a situation that could be exacerbated by decisions made in London. Such decisions could affect the stability of the region and hence British interests in the West Indies at a time of conflict with its greatest enemy, the French. The letter was written, of course, just a few days before the vote in the House of Commons which rejected the bill for abolition of the slave trade, the outcome of which was unknown to Nelson. His comment about the slave trade is, therefore, more a reflection about the potential military consequences of abolition at that time rather than any implied support for the trade.

The Barbary Slave Trade

In December 1799 Nelson wrote to The Honourable William Wyndham, Secretary at War in Pitt's government, in the following terms:

'*I am this moment favoured with your letter of November 21st: and my blood boils that I cannot chastise these Pirates. They could not show themselves in the Mediterranean, did our country not permit. Never let us talk of the cruelty of the African Slave Trade, while we permit such a horrid war...*'[48]

The 'horrid war' which Nelson is referring to is the Barbary slave trade. Nelson goes on to say, in clear recognition of the limit of his influence and powers that, even with the fleet at his disposal, he could not take action to prevent it without plunging the country into a war which (British) merchants would hate and in which Ministers would not support him. It is clear from the tone of his letter that Nelson was familiar with the arguments about the cruelty of slavery and he equates the Barbary slave trade with the African Atlantic slave trade. His comment is, effectively, why act on one and not the other. Although not on the same scale as the African slave trade, it is estimated that the Barbary slave trade took over one and a quarter million people into slavery, from a wide range of national and ethnic backgrounds.

The Mediterranean was, at the time, Nelson's theatre of war. (After his stunning victory at the Battle of the Nile he was mortified that Lord Keith was given command of the Mediterranean over him, after the retirement of Earl St Vincent). In October 1799 the English Consul in Tripoli advised Nelson that the Bashaw (generally a man of high rank in northern Africa) was not averse to peace with Naples but wanted to know what sum he would receive 'as he has Neopolitan slaves'. Further the Bashaw advised he would need to declare war on some other nation or lay up his cruizers. A very good reason for being at war, Nelson noted sarcastically![49]

Nelson had written to the Earl Spencer, at the end of November 1799 advising that the situation with the Barbary States called for serious attention.[50] He described how Maltese and Neapolitan vessels would not go to sea without a 'pass' signed by himself, although he had serious doubts about the worth of such passes. The passes were generally respected by Tripoli and Tunis but not by the Algerine cruizers (sic) who stopped merchantmen, seized their vessels and cargo and took their crews into slavery. Nelson's proposal was to go to the Dey of Algiers (a ruler of the Regency of Algiers) 'to settle the business', by force if necessary. As part of this approach Nelson would insist that the Dey should not keep the 'poor people in slavery'. Nelson was anxious to know the sentiments of the government on this issue.

In his letter to Wyndham he says 'my heart bleeds' and pleads for the necessary orders from Government to enable him to 'chastise these Pirates'. The matter rumbled on and Nelson duly wrote to the Dey of Algiers noting that ships benefitting from his 'pass' had been taken and many persons had been carried into slavery. Nelson made it clear that the ships were carrying provisions to help the fight against the common enemy – France – and sought the immediate release of those 'poor people' who, due to his pass, put themselves in the power of the Dey.

The issue of the Barbary slave trade was a constant concern to Nelson. He had cause to write to the Bey of Tunis (the governor of the province) in December 1799 in similar terms to those sent to the Dey of Algiers. Again he sought to use his reputation to secure the release of 'those poor men who were taken by your cruizers, taking provisions to the Island of Malta'. Nelson made it clear that his 'pass' was only given to vessels carrying provisions for Britain's ships of war and not to vessels for trade. He hoped these considerations would result in the release of those 'poor men and their vessels'. In March 1800 Nelson wrote to the Bashaw of Tripoli and advised him that he had rescued 'many of your subjects from a French prison', whom he released following the capture of *Le Genereux* (one of only two French ships to escape the Battle of the Nile) off Malta.

Against this background it is not surprising that, in his letter to Wyndham, Nelson shows his exasperation that the Government were devoting their energies to the African slave trade but, in essence, ignoring the Barbary slave trade which was having an immediate effect on the theatre of war with which he was concerned. It was, of course, expedient and necessary for Nelson to seek the release of vessels and their crews, but there is no doubting that he felt deeply the cruelties of this slave trade, and there is no reason to suppose that he felt differently about the African slave trade. That he did not opine on this is perhaps a reflection of the fact that he was not directly confronted by it. His dealings with the Barbary Pirates also illustrate that, despite his reputation in the wake of the Battle of the Nile, he was aware of the limit of his influence on matters beyond the naval realm.

Sir John Duckworth and Saint-Domingue

(Note: Saint-Domingue, also referred to in texts and correspondence as St Domingo, or San Domingo, is the western part of the island of Hispaniola (now Haiti and the Dominican Republic) in the Greater Antilles in the Caribbean. This part of the island, which now forms the republic of Haiti, was ceded to France in 1697 when it named it Saint-Domingue. To avoid confusion, and for the sake of consistency, I have adopted Saint-Domingue as the name, where relevant, of this part of the island. In reproducing letters, and/or transcripts of them, of the period I have retained original spellings).

Sir John Duckworth began his naval career at the age of 11 and served in the Seven Years' War, the American War of Independence and the French Revolutionary and Napoleonic Wars.

After the declaration of war between France and Great Britain in May 1803 the Royal Navy sent a squadron, under the leadership of Sir John Duckworth, to Jamaica, where he assumed control of the Jamaica Station as Commander-in-Chief. His task was to capture or destroy French warships and sever communication between French outposts in the region.

In December 1803 Duckworth led a negotiation with the French forces at Saint-Domingue, soon to become the world's first independent black republic, Haiti, which by then was almost entirely under the control of the black revolutionary forces. This resulted in the surrender of the French General Rochambeau and his troops who were taken as prisoners of war to Jamaica (see also below pp 74-75). Nelson wrote to Duckworth on 10th March 1803 congratulating him on his success.[51] He went on to say:

'Now you have done with the French, unless you can get hold by agreement with the sold Spaniards, of their part of St Domingo, (for I hope in God we shall never attempt to possess any portion of the other part of that Island,) although I see all the danger of a Black Republic, yet I trust we shall be very particular in making a treaty of commerce with them'.[52]

At the time of writing this letter the eventually successful revolt by self-freed slaves on the French-controlled part of the island of Saint-Domingue was nearing a conclusion. General Rochambeau had led a vicious campaign against the revolutionaries but defeat was near and he surrendered to the British. In the letter Nelson refers to the prospect of securing the Spanish-controlled eastern part of the island by negotiation, but is clear that he hopes Britain will not attempt to try and possess the 'other part' of the island i.e. that part under the control of the freed slaves, which subsequently became Haiti, the world's first Black Republic, in 1804. Nelson would have been aware of the significant loss of life on both sides which occurred in the fight for Haiti's independence, and would also have known that the freed slaves had successfully defeated European forces, including those from Britain. Hence his concern that Britain should never attempt to possess any part of the new state.

The 'dangers' of a Black Republic (which at the time was near to fruition), to which Nelson alludes, are likely to be the possible incitements to, and support for, slave revolts elsewhere in the (British) West Indies which would, in turn, de-stabilise the region and divert resources away from the main conflict with the French in Europe. It is interesting to note, though, Nelson's pragmatic view that a commercial treaty with the new republic should be pursued – a recognition of the new state and a 'normalising' of relations –which might avert the dangers perceived.

5

CONCLUSIONS TO PART ONE

A careful assessment of the allegations made in *The Guardian* clearly shows that those contentions are ill-founded. There is no evidence to show that Nelson used his seat in the House of Lords or his 'influence' to perpetuate the slave trade and its attendant horrors.

Nelson was, of course, duty bound to support and protect the instruments of state, as a king's officer and through his allegiance and commitment to his chosen profession, the Royal Navy. Part of those instruments of state was the colonial system which was, in turn, underpinned by the slave trade. As a senior naval officer Nelson was unlikely to challenge the status quo. Whilst bound to support the slave trade (until abolished by law), the Admiralty view of the treatment of slaves on board ship was significantly more liberal, essentially according slaves the same rights as other seamen. So whilst Nelson would not and could not act to the detriment of the expressed national interest he would have been exposed to the Navy's more liberal regime. Notwithstanding that Nelson was driven by duty and a thirst for glory, he was always bound by the directives of his superiors.

A number of examples exist which demonstrate that Nelson, when confronted with the issue of slavery, behaved in a humane and compassionate way. In addition there is no suggestion or nuance in the many thousands of letters which Nelson wrote, and which are a key source of his thoughts, to suggest he was racist or, as alleged, a 'white supremacist' in the modern sense. It would have been difficult for anyone holding those views to conceal them, especially as (for much of Nelson's lifetime) there was no particular censure for expressing them. Indeed the expression of such views was commonplace elsewhere. In addition it is clear that Nelson had valued relationships with persons of different ethnicities and at no point were these relationships 'exceptional' i.e. his judgement of people was based on their merits rather than their skin colour.

The evidence suggests that Nelson, unlike many of his contemporaries, believed in a meritocracy and judged people on their character and abilities rather than the colour of their skin.

Nelson's post mortem reputation has clouded judgement on the true, limited extent of his influence on the major (non-naval) issues of the day.

Looked at through the prism of 21st century morality, Nelson's greatest fault, perhaps, is that he did not use his reputation to influence the debate opposing the slave trade which his actions would suggest he leant towards, as he generally kept his own counsel on this issue.[53]Further he has been accused of only intervening in slave related issues when it was expedient to do so.[54] However these criticisms overlook the reality of Nelson's position and status as a serving naval officer. He was not in a position to speak openly on matters of government policy. To have done so would undoubtedly have led to serious admonishment. Nelson cannot be condemned for supporting the status quo, which was his role in life and which helped him achieve his personal ambitions of fame, glory and public adulation.

There is, of course, one further issue to be addressed – Nelson's letter to Simon Taylor which has been construed as defining Nelson's view on the slave trade and race. That letter is the subject of Part Two of this book.

PART TWO:DECEIT

'History is affected by discoveries we may make in the future' Karl Popper, Philosopher

6

NELSON'S LETTERS

In this part of the study, one of Nelson's letters is considered in detail. That letter is an important one in the discussion of Nelson and slavery. It is the letter which Nelson penned to Simon Taylor of Jamaica in June 1805.

Consideration of this letter raises a significant dilemma. That is, the extent to which reliance can be placed on the printed sources of Nelson's letters.

The most extensive collection of published Nelson letters is the seven volume series edited by Sir Nicholas Harris Nicolas entitled *The Dispatches and Letters of Vice Admiral Lord Viscount Nelson* (first published between 1844 and 1846).[1] However, Nicolas notes in the Preface to Volume 1, that he did not always have access to primary sources but rather he often relied upon the versions of the letters reproduced in Clarke and McArthurs' *The Life and Services of Horatio Viscount Nelson*(1809 and second edition of 1840). However, Clark and McArthur, amongst Nelson's earliest biographers, were often selective in their choice of passages and frequently re-worded and edited the letters to which they referred, to reflect the grammatical conventions of the day. More significantly, some transcriptions were altered, seemingly to avoid embarrassment to establishment figures whose names were removed in the published letters.

Nicolas, in turn, made limited amendments to the punctuation and orthography of the letters but, inevitably, imported adaptations and/or omissions of those earlier published letters. In addition, he admits to suppressing certain letters, such as Nelson's letters to Lady Hamilton. Caution must therefore be exercised in relying upon the versions of Nelson's letters published after his death.

HMS *Victory* off Martinique, 10th June 1805

We can imagine Nelson in his cabin, sitting at his writing desk. He is agitated and unhappy. He has pursued the French and Spanish fleets across the Atlantic but has not yet brought them to battle. He is agitated because he undertook this venture without express orders from the Admiralty and he needs to show good cause for doing so. He is unhappy because he believes he was given false intelligence, which he attributes to Brigadier-General Brereton in St Lucia, who misled him in his pursuit 'and deprived us of a Battle'.[2]

About this time Nelson had learned that a friend, the Reverend Dr Scott, had lost his living as Rector of St John's in Jamaica. To try and help his friend restore his living Nelson decides to write to an old acquaintance on Jamaica, Simon Taylor. However, Nelson has not corresponded with Taylor for several years, so to set a favourable tone for his request, Nelson at first describes the actions he has taken to defend the West Indies and then panders to Taylor's prejudices by affirming his support for the colonial system and his disdain for Wilberforce. Upon completing this letter he makes a copy for personal record purposes.

Two days later, off Antigua, Nelson settles down to write to William Marsden, at the Admiralty. In his letter he bemoans the bad intelligence but, in mitigation, claims to have 'saved' some two hundred and upwards merchant sugar ships and their cargoes. He wrote in similar terms to Prince William Henry and added a footnote about the sugar ships in a short letter to his agent, Alexander Davison.[3]

Who was Simon Taylor?[4]

Simon Taylor (1740-1813) was one of the wealthiest plantation and slaveholders in the West Indies. He was born in Kingston, Jamaica and, not untypically, was educated at Eton (1752-55). He inherited a substantial fortune upon the death of his father and devoted his life to developing this fortune. He retained a strong affinity with Jamaica and, unlike many of the planter class, he remained settled on the island throughout his life, dying there in 1813.

Taylor owned several plantations on the eastern side of the island and he also acted as a manager for several more. Taylor was a representative of the Jamaican Legislative Assembly and was active in objecting to proposals for the abolition of the slave trade and slavery itself. Taylor never married but had at least one 'housekeeper/mistress', Grace Donne, a free woman of colour. When he died, Taylor was the richest planter in Jamaica owning over 2000 slaves and a substantial personal fortune, as well as significant property and other assets, which made him one of the wealthiest men in the British Empire at the time. Of course, such an assessment does not give any clue to the exploitation, violence, de-humanisation and misery involved in the making of that fortune through the continued use of slave labour and the slave trade.

The West Indian planters looked to Britain for support and stability and were severely shaken by the American colonies seeking independence from Britain, with which they felt closely integrated. Declaring their loyalty to Britain the West Indian planters were further shaken by the proposals for the abolition of slavery, which challenged their presumption that only white persons could enjoy the full rights of being English/British. They called on all of their influential contacts to thwart the movement. In 1783 the West India planters and associated commercial interests had formed a lobbying group to represent them in London where policies were emerging at odds with their political and economic ambitions. This group was known as the London West India Committee and drew on close associations with absentee plantation owners, some of whom were members of Parliament. Between 1785 and 1807 nearly one third of the Committee's meetings were devoted to discussing the proposals for the abolition of the slave trade and devising a campaign to thwart the legislation. Simon Taylor chaired the Committee on several occasions. Jamaica was also the best represented colony in a Standing Committee of the group, its aim being the development of a lobbying strategy, and its implementation.

The loyalty of the planters to the Crown was being severely tested. They felt betrayed by the noises coming out of London and they were further troubled by the revolutionary fervour finding a voice in France. Taylor was no exception. He fed pro-slavery material to supportive voices in London in an effort to thwart the abolitionist charge, arguing that abolition would result in a threat to the Empire and the national interest. The planters further argued that the abolition of slavery would provide France with a strategic advantage in the Caribbean region – a threat which was, of course, significantly reduced, if not removed, by Nelson's victory at Trafalgar. Taylor was bitterly stung by the abolition of the slave trade and grew increasingly ill, withdrawing from public life on Jamaica. He died on April 14th 1813.

A Curious Discovery

Shortly after Nelson's death, a purported copy of Nelson's letter to Simon Taylor was in circulation. That copy letter was discovered in 2018 by Martyn Downer, an avid researcher, author and leading specialist in artefacts and material relating to Lord Nelson. Initially put aside as a curiosity, as the letter was clearly not in Nelson's handwriting, the letter's importance was not realised until the current debate about Nelson and the slave trade took hold. (A note on Nelson's handwriting can be found in Appendix 12). The letter is now in the possession of the National Museum of the Royal Navy (NMRN) in Portsmouth and is referred to hereinafter as the NMRN version.

At the end of 2018, the *BBC History Magazine* published the article by Christer Petley which concluded that Nelson was a committed supporter of the slave trade.[5] That article relied on yet another version of the Nelson-Taylor letter. That is, one which was published in Cobbett's *Political Register* in 1807. The differences between the NMRN copy and the Cobbett version aroused suspicion that Nelson's original letter had been altered. The Cobbett version also differed from the version of the letter subsequently published in Nicolas. The only way of checking which, if any, of these versions accurately reflected Nelson's original letter, would be to find that original, which had not surfaced.

Then, in 2020, a reference to the letter was found in John Sugden's *'Sword of Albion'*. This hinted that a 'pressed' copy of the original letter resided in the British Library. Frustratingly, due to the national Covid-19 pandemic, access to the manuscript section of the British Library was restricted and it was not until later that year that access was possible. It was only when the letter could be viewed that the extent of differences between it and other versions could be determined.

Nelson's 'Pressed' Letters

The manuscript section of the British Library in London houses a little- researched collection of nine volumes of 'pressed copy' letters. Pressed copies of original letters were obtained by using a specially designed machine to press damp tissue paper on to the original letter, giving a mirror image. This was then reversed so the text could be read through the tissue paper. This impression was then stuck on to light grey paper so that the text could be more clearly read. The pressed letters are direct copies of original letters written by Admiral

Fig 7: William Cobbett.

Lord Nelson and which form part of a Nelson archive known as the Bridport Papers. Dr Colin White analysed the archive and concluded that many of the letters were not recorded elsewhere, many being unpublished at the time he undertook his research. White noted that some of the unpublished letters were of a private or personal nature or concerned with secret diplomatic and intelligence matters. This suggests that Nelson and his staff retained these copy letters which were deemed inappropriate for inclusion in official letter books. There are nearly 1100 letters in the Bridport collection and one of them, the letter written to Simon Taylor, is at the epicentre of the current debate surrounding Nelson's reputation.

The content of this letter is alleged to support claims that Nelson was pro-slavery but, as will be seen, the letter was embellished and tampered with, in essence forged, by the anti-abolitionist, pro-slavery movement after Nelson's death. This was an attempt to use Nelson's burgeoning posthumous reputation to influence the debates in Parliament on the abolition of the slave trade in 1807.

The Letter

Below is a transcript of the pressed letter as contained in the Bridport Papers (original spelling and punctuation is maintained) and as viewed once the pandemic allowed.[6] The original letter appears to have been lost or destroyed and consequently the pressed letter is the earliest, extant and true copy of the letter. The Bridport pressed letter is reproduced on paper bearing an 1802 watermark and its authenticity is not in doubt. It is the copy letter which Nelson instructed his secretary to make on June 10th 1805. The letter details Nelson's actions in seeking to protect the West Indies, and then re-affirms his commitment to the protection of the Colonies. The pressed letter is reproduced in Appendix 1.

This letter is critical in trying to ascertain Nelson's views on the slave trade, slavery and colonialism. It therefore warrants detailed consideration.

'Victory June 10 1805
My Dear Sir
I was in a thousand fears for Jamaica for that is a blow which Bonaparte would be happy to give us, I had no hesitation in forming my judgement, and I flew to the West Indies without any orders, but I think the Ministry cannot be displeased. Information at Barbadoes from St Lucia told us that the enemys squadron had sailed with 5000 troops on May 28th: and were seen standing to the Southward, therefore Tobago, Trinidad or Grenada was supposed their object, I went to those islands but now I find it was the whole a fabrication for that the enemy did not leave Port Royal till the night of June 5th on the 6th were under Dominica, on the 7th under Guadalope, standing to the North, and supposed either to try and carry Antigua or were trying to escape from me. The Carthegena squadron was at sea but returned on hearing I was close to them, therefore they had no troops on board that would make our Jamaican friends alarmed, when I am satisfied

that they are on their return after sending some of the Spanish ships to the Havannah I shall push hard to get off the straits mouth before them and kind providence may some happy day bless my endeavours to serve the Public of which the West India Colonies form so prominent and interesting a part, I ever have been and shall die a firm friend of our present colonial system. I was bred as you know in the Good old school and taught to appreciate the value of our West India possessions, and neither in the field or the Senate shall their just rights be infringed whilst I have an arm to fight in their defence or a tongue to launch my voice against the damnable cruel doctrine of Wilberforce and his Hipocritical allies and I hope that my birth in Heaven will be as exalted as his, who would certainly cause the murder of all our friends and fellow subjects in the colonies, however I did not intend to have gone so far but the sentiments are full in my breast and the pen would write them

I shall as soon as I have done with their fleet go to England for a few months and if you have time and inclination I should be very glad to hear from you, we are nearly thirty years acquaintance and am ever my dear Mr Taylor your faithful and obliged friend & servant

Nelson & Bronte

The Revd Dr Scott Rector of St Johns Jamaica is a most staunch friend to Jamaica and I am sorry to find he has lost his living by some new law. The Dr desires his best remembrances and good wishes to you. He is a worthy good man and a very old friend of mine, If any of my Jamaica friends are near you I beg to be kindly remembered to them'

For the purposes of this study the key part of the letter really begins with the phrase 'I ever have been ..' and concludes with 'fellow subjects in the colonies'. In this section of the letter Nelson states that he is a firm friend of the present colonial system and that he was taught the value of the West India possessions. He goes on to state that 'neither in the field or the senate shall their just rights'(of those colonies) be infringed whilst he has an arm to fight or voice to speak against the damnable cruel doctrine of Wilberforce and his hypocritical allies who would certainly cause the murder of all our friends and fellow subjects in the colonies. This passage of the letter, upon which those who accuse Nelson of being anti-abolitionist/pro-slavery rely, does, on the face of it, seem quite damning. However, its contents are strangely inconsistent with Nelson's actions and other utterances. Indeed, there seems to be little other corroborating evidence that Nelson opposed the abolition of the slave trade or was otherwise pro-slavery. So this begs the question as to why Nelson expressed himself in this way.

At the time that Nelson wrote this letter, the Government was being publicly attacked for neglecting the interests of the West Indies and possibly laying them open to attacks by the French. The letter was aimed, in part, at allaying public fears in the West Indies on this point. By writing to Taylor, a prominent Jamaican, Nelson could be assured that the message, that he was being vigorous in his pursuit of the French and protection of the colonies, would be spread.

The letter is carefully worded and intended as private correspondence.[7] The first part of the letter, which deals with naval matters, is couched in Nelson's usual vainglorious terms: (the enemy were) 'trying to escape from **me**' and 'on hearing **I** was close to them' (returned to Havannah).In the second part of the letter Nelson affirms his support for the colonial system. At the time of writing this letter Nelson would have been cognisant of proposals to retain the colonies whilst reforming the system of slavery to provide rights to enslaved peoples, and of his own support for one such proposal, by Lieutenant Layman RN which is considered in detail below.

It should be noted that, in his letter, Nelson does not expressly support slavery or the slave trade which, as will be seen, is a fact of singular importance. The Nelson-Taylor letter contains a number of key phrases, careful consideration of which helps in understanding Nelson's intent and meaning in respect of this letter. These phrases include: the 'Good old school', 'just rights', 'damnable cruel doctrine', and 'Wilberforce and his hypocritical allies'.

The 'Good old school'

There is no doubt that during the 18th, 19th and 20th centuries Britain was a colonial power and that during the 18th and early 19th century particularly the slave trade was seen by some as an essential component of that colonial system. The West Indies were critical to the Atlantic economy in the 18th century with sugar central to imports from the Caribbean to Britain during that period, accounting for some 18.5% of British trade from 1758 to 1817.[8] The value of the sugar industry was such that protection of the West Indian colonies was seen as vital to the safeguarding of the British economy and consequently meant the region was under constant threat from other (colonial) powers. Clearly only the Royal Navy could protect the Caribbean island colonies from external threats. The largest and most valuable of these colonies was Jamaica. If the Royal Navy lost command of the seas then the colonies could be lost, as was so critically demonstrated at the loss of Yorktown during the American War of Independence.

During the global Seven Years War (1756-63) the Caribbean became the focus of much naval activity and a number of battles, and 'the myth of British naval supremacy became a reality' during this period.[9] The Seven Years War established the Royal Navy as the dominant European naval power and sealed the navy's role as the main protector of the Caribbean islands. Without the colonies, Britain did not have the wealth to maintain such wars. The naval officer became a role model as the exemplar for 'Britishness' with the virtues of loyalty, honour, liberty, grace and courage.[10] This is the 'Good old school' into which a youthful Nelson was introduced. It is inevitable that he would have been inculcated with these values during his years of education in the Navy, having finished his formal education at the age of 12. Indeed, in his own account of his services (his autobiography) Nelson concludes that 'perseverance in any profession will most probably meet its own reward … I have received all the honours of my profession … and I may say to the reader "go thou and do likewise".[11]

Nelson clearly placed these old school values at the centre of his being. To these values can be added 'duty', even more so after the Admiral Byng affair.[12] Duty was the over-riding driving force of Nelson's career as is exemplified in his final signal at the Battle of Trafalgar – 'England Expects That Every Man Will Do His Duty'. Indeed, amongst his final words, repeated several times were 'Thank God I have done my duty'. To Nelson the concept of 'duty' was wide ranging. It was not limited to just obeying orders. It embraced a responsibility for protecting Britain's interests and reputation and enforcing her laws.

The American War of Independence had a serious effect on the West Indian colonists with whom reciprocal trade was significant. The Navy's role after the war was to enforce the Navigation Acts, which Nelson strongly upheld, whilst other naval officers turned a blind eye to such trade. Nelson's world view was clearly at odds with that of the islanders and, as he noted in his 'autobiography', he put into practice his professional ('old school') views: ".... I proved ... that a captain of a man-of-war is in duty bound to support all maritime laws, by his admiralty commission alone, without becoming a custom-house officer". Again this express statement of his philosophy showed he felt duty bound to support the (colonial) system which he was sent to defend, and in which significant resources were expended, reflecting the value of the colonies to Britain's global power. The role of the Navy was to protect Britain's colonies and Nelson would have known (have been taught) the value of those possessions to the British crown. His comments to Taylor in the letter are therefore fully consistent with his perceived professional role.

'Just Rights'

Nelson states he would not see the 'just rights' of the West India possessions infringed. Nelson's duty was to protect British interests as defined by Parliament, as an officer in the Royal Navy and by his oath of allegiance given to the King as a member of the House of Lords. But, of course, those just rights could be changed by law and Nelson, sensitive to the changing scene, would have been aware of the debates regarding the extent to which the British Government wielded power over the colonies, as well as the abolitionist proposals in Parliament. At the time Nelson penned his letter the slave trade and slavery, reprehensible as they were, were still legal. The scope of the 'just rights' might change, but Nelson was, and felt, duty bound to uphold them, so his use of this term can be regarded as carefully considered.

William Wilberforce and Nelson: 'a damnable cruel doctrine' and 'hypocritical allies'.

William Wilberforce (1759-1833) is best known as the leader of the anti-slavery movement. He entered Parliament in 1780 and in 1785 became an evangelical Christian which resulted in a lifelong concern for reform. He championed campaigns such as the Society for the Suppression of Vice and Encouragement of Religion, the Society for the Prevention of Cruelty to Animals, and the foundation of the Church Mission Society. He headed the Parliamentary campaigns against the slave trade for some 20 years, resulting in the abolition of the slave trade in 1807. He continued his support for the complete abolition of slavery even after stepping down from Parliament in 1826. He died just three days after the passing of the Slavery Abolition Act in 1833.

In 1776 Wilberforce attended St John's College, Cambridge, where he pursued a hedonistic lifestyle of gambling and drinking. It was here that he met the future Prime Minister, William Pitt and, in 1780, at the age of 21, Wilberforce was elected to Parliament, representing Kingston upon Hull. In 1787 Wilberforce met with Thomas Clarkson, a dedicated abolitionist who sought a commitment from Wilberforce to bring forward the case for the abolition of the slave trade in the House of Commons. Wilberforce began his Parliamentary campaign in 1789 although he acceded to a request by the anti-abolitionists that the House of Commons heard its own evidence, a move to which Wilberforce agreed, and for which he was subsequently criticised. A Parliamentary sub-committee was set up in 1790 to hear the considerable mass of evidence. (It was to this sub-committee that Hercules Ross gave evidence). In 1791 Wilberforce introduced a bill to abolish the slave trade which was defeated by 163 votes to 88, probably as a result of events in revolutionary France and slave revolts in the French West Indies.

In 1793 another vote to abolish the slave trade was narrowly defeated but the outbreak of war with France led to politicians' attention being deflected from the issue and it was not until the early years of the 19th century that public and political interest in the matter increased. In June 1804 Wilberforce's bill to abolish the slave trade successfully passed through the Commons, although it was too late in the session of Parliament to complete its passage through the Lords. When re-introduced for the 1805 session it was defeated. In the general election of 1806 the abolition of the slave trade became an election issue and in February 1807 the bill was carried (despite the anti-abolitionists' attempt to influence matters by using Nelson's posthumous reputation and a doctored copy of Nelson's letter to Simon Taylor).

Fig 8: William Wilberforce.

The Act received Royal Assent on 25th March 1807.

For his persistence in pushing through the abolition of the slave trade, history has accorded Wilberforce the accolade of being the hero of the anti-slavery movement. However, Nelson, along with many of his contemporaries, found Wilberforce to be hypocritical and divisive. The sources of this derision are easy to find. Wilberforce was very often at the forefront of government repression and opposition to workers' rights. For example, Wilberforce supported the 1794 Habeas Corpus Suspension Act which allowed the government to imprison people whilst removing their right to challenge the lawfulness of that detention[13]. He also supported Acts aimed at curbing freedom of speech, assembly and organisation, and he spoke in favour of the Combination Act in 1799, an Act which suppressed trade union activity, calling unions 'a general disease in our society'. Wilberforce's reputation, if not all of these actions, would have been known to Nelson. Seen in the context of a broad naval education and professional ethos, Nelson's comments about Wilberforce are hardly surprising. So, at the time, Wilberforce, whilst promoting the abolition of slavery, stood against the improvement of workers' rights in Britain, hence Nelson's assertion of his and his followers' hypocrisy. These actions led to accusations that Wilberforce 'never favoured the liberty of any white man in his life' and to Hazlitt condemning him as someone 'who preaches vital Christianity to untutored savages, and tolerates its worst abuses in civilised states'.[14] William Cobbett called him the prince of hypocrites who praised the benefits of poverty from a comfortable distance.[15] (Wilberforce was the beneficiary of an extensive fortune which he used in aid of a number of 'good causes'). Wilberforce's avocation of the abolition of the slave trade was seen in stark contrast to his views on workers' rights in England, and hence the accusation of hypocrisy. William Cobbett said of Wilberforce 'Never have you done one single act in favour of the labourers of this country'. There is a strange and ironic symmetry here; Wilberforce was a conservative who opposed workers' rights in Britain whilst promoting the abolition of the slave trade and subsequently slavery, whilst Cobbett was a radical who fought for workers' rights but was pro-slavery.

Nelson, like Wilberforce and the majority of the British people at the time, was essentially conservative in his views. Unsurprisingly, for a parson's son, religion was very much at the centre of his beliefs. His basic philosophy was of a paternalistic society, where caring masters would look after their charges in return for loyalty and obedience, a principle which applied particularly on board his ships. Consequently Nelson was generally opposed to anyone seeking to alter the balance of the constitution where, as he saw it, a benign monarch ruled wisely but with accountability to the Lords and the Commons. Sir William Hamilton, who knew Nelson well, described him as being 'of a liberal persuasion' – his paternalism embraced a sympathy for those struggling to survive. In contrast to Wilberforce, he was prepared to speak up on their behalf especially where he saw their condition as a failing of the ruling classes. Nowhere is this better exemplified than when, 'on the beach' in 1792, Nelson brought the 'distressing poverty' of the rural poor in Norfolk to the attention of the Duke of Clarence. ('On the beach' is term which applied to officers of the navy who were stood down from active duty, particularly in times of peace. They were on land rather than on-board ship. During such periods they were generally retained on half pay). In a letter to the Duke he made it clear that the poor 'are really in need of everything to make life comfortable' and that this situation had arisen 'from the neglect of the country gentlemen' in failing to raise wages as the price of necessities had increased. To support his argument Nelson included in the letter a detailed analysis of income and expenditure for a labourer with a wife and three children, and this at a time when Nelson was on half pay and by no means affluent himself. (In later years he made regular contributions to help needy parishioners in Burnham Thorpe). It seems likely that Nelson's view of Wilberforce was influenced by Wilberforce's stance on such domestic matters.

In his letter to Simon Taylor in June 1805 Nelson referred to Wilberforce 'and his hypocritical allies' and his 'damnable cruel doctrine'. The latter phrase was subsequently altered by the anti-abolitionists to 'damnable and cursed doctrine'. If Nelson was, by all accounts, a humanitarian in his philosophy and deeds, and someone who put religion in a central position in his life – for example he ensured that all cabins in his ships were furnished with a bible – then why would he find Wilberforce's call for the abolition of the slave trade to be 'cruel'? The answer lies in the events that occurred on the French occupied part of the island of Saint-Domingue. The western part of the island (now Haiti) was controlled by the French and was separated from the Spanish controlled eastern part of the island by a significant mountain range.

Saint-Domingue was the largest and richest of the West Indian colonies, with some 425,000 black slaves, 40,000 whites and 28,000 mulattoes and free blacks in the early 1790s. A revolt by self-liberated slaves began in August 1791 and ended with the colony's independence on 1st January 1804. The revolution was particularly bloody with atrocities committed on both sides, and it is estimated that it cost the lives of some 200,000 blacks and 50,000 Europeans as well as thousands of mulattoes. Matters escalated in 1802 with the French leader, Vicomte de Rochambeau, leading a vicious campaign against the revolutionaries. His savagery was matched by the Haitians under

Jean-Jacques Dessalines.[16] Following a number of atrocities and fearful of a similar revolution in Jamaica, Simon Taylor wrote to Nelson in October 1802, seeking aid and assistance in supporting the case of the colonial planters in Parliament.

Taylor made specific reference to the events in Saint-Domingue noting the 'scene it now presents .... 20,000 negroes and mulattoes, as well as 3000 white people butchered, massacred and murdered, in consequence of the dream of liberty' (see endnote[17] and Appendix 11). Taylor goes on to ascribe a financial cost to the revolution and gives graphic descriptions of some of the atrocities.

Prompted more by criticism that the government was neglecting the protection of the West Indies, and by his desire to assist his friend, Revd Dr Scott, Nelson wrote to Taylor from HMS *Victory* in June 1805. It is also likely that Nelson had more up to date intelligence of the revolt in Saint-Domingue. In 1803 Nelson was appointed Commander-in-Chief of the Mediterranean fleet, a post he coveted, and he set sail from Portsmouth on 20th May. On 28th May HMS *Victory* captured, without a fight, the *Ambuscade,* a French frigate returning to France from the West Indies. The *Ambuscade* had been captured at the end of 1798 from the Royal Navy, to which she was now returned. On board were 23 prisoners, amongst them General Chretien, a black Haitian revolutionary officer, and his servant. Chretien and his servant volunteered to serve with Nelson during his stay in the Mediterranean or until he had action with the enemy. On 19th April 1805 (i.e. before his letter to Simon Taylor) Nelson wrote to William Marsden at the Admiralty asking him to honour the discharge of Chretien and his servant, and to pay them the 'wages due to them' and to assist them in returning to the West Indies, either to Jamaica or Saint-Domingue. Nelson then states: 'The particular attention shown the said General may have a good effect, and hereafter be of great advantage, in case of disturbances at Jamaica, or any other of our West India Islands'.[18]

Nelson had clearly discussed the Saint-Domingue situation with General Chretien and he hoped his humane and reasonable treatment of him would help avert disturbances on the British islands. The knowledge gained, backed by his inherent conservatism and belief in the stability of the existing order, would lead Nelson to conclude that Wilberforce's doctrine was indeed cruel, as he believed it would lead to outcomes similar to those on Saint-Domingue, ('the murder of all our friends and fellow subjects') where all sides suffered the brutality of the revolution. It should be remembered that the Navigation Acts had been amended to include slaves in the West Indies as being British (subjects) and Nelson, very knowledgeable of those Acts, intended slaves to be included in his concerns.

The timing of Nelson's letter to Taylor is also important in understanding Nelson's views. The abolition of the slave trade would still leave slaves in the colonies. Wilberforce's hope was that the abolition of the slave trade would lead to a more humane treatment of the slaves in the colonies, creating conditions where slave communities would become self-sustaining. This is in stark contrast to another proposal supported by Nelson which would see slaves replaced by 'industrious' Chinese labour (see 'Nelson and Layman' p101 below).

At the time Nelson penned his letter to Taylor, Britain itself was under the threat of invasion by Napoleon who had amassed a significant number of troops in northern France for that purpose, an invasion ambition ultimately thwarted by the Royal Navy's blockade of the channel ports. Victory at Trafalgar, only a few months later, finally put an end to Napoleon's ambition to invade Britain. If a slave revolt occurred in the West Indies it was unlikely that resources could be diverted to protect the colonial interest, making an outcome of chaos and violence, such as that in Saint-Domingue, more likely. This fear significantly qualifies Nelson's alleged support for the slave trade, as inferred by others from the letter to Simon Taylor.

For these military and humane reasons Nelson states his opposition to Wilberforce's doctrine at that critical time.

There are several ironies in the disdain in which Nelson held Wilberforce. Upon hearing of Nelson's death, Wilberforce 'was so overcome with grief that he could not go on reading for tears'.[19] Further, in 1806 when the issue of an allowance for Nelson's successors to his title was discussed on several occasions in Parliament, Hansard reports Wilberforce's statement that the grant was not so much as a provision for Nelson's family but 'held out to our navy to encourage an imitation of that hero's example'. It is clear that Wilberforce held Nelson in high regard, and his eulogy suggests that he had not heard any whisperings in the corridors of Parliament about Nelson holding pro-slavery or anti-abolitionist views. Wilberforce would later (1807) have been aware of the version of the Nelson-Taylor letter published in Cobbett's *Political Register* with his (Wilberforce's) name edited out, but this does not appear to have altered his views of Nelson. Indeed, the letter does not appear to have been referred to in the subsequent debates in Parliament. Judgement should probably be left to those who knew Nelson best and Wilberforce would undoubtedly have known him better than any modern commentator.

7

FORGERIES EXPOSED

It was only when access to the Bridport collection was possible, in 2020, and the pressed copy of Nelson's original letter found, that the suspicion that a conspiracy to adapt (forge) Nelson's letter to support the anti-abolitionists' cause could be confirmed.

The NMRN letter has a fabricated Nelson and Bronte signature and portrait seal which were presumably for public display. The letter is reproduced on paper watermarked 1798. This version is, in essence, a forgery and was made by the pro-slavery lobby in Jamaica for circulation in London in an attempt to use Nelson's reputation to influence debates in Parliament on the abolition of the slave trade in their favour. The original of Nelson's letter (the true, pressed copy of which is found in the Bridport collection) seems to have been lost or was most likely destroyed at some point to prevent the extent of changes made to it, by the anti-abolitionists, being discovered. There is circumstantial evidence, however, to suggest that it may have been in existence as late as 1831. Nelson himself, of course, was dead and unable to explain the meaning of the letter or challenge the changes.

The handwriting of the pressed letter and the NMRN forgery are clearly and obviously different (see Appendices 1 and 2). The content of the NMRN copy of Nelson's letter also differs in several subtle but none the less significant ways from the original letter. Indeed, some 25 or so changes and additions to the original letter can be detected. Some of these are seemingly minor 'editorial' changes, although other changes appear designed to influence the reader's interpretation of Nelson's views. For example, in the Bridport letter Nelson states he was 'in a thousand fears' for Jamaica. The NMRN copy changes the word 'fears' to 'cares'. At first sight this does not seem important. The word 'fears' conveys a sense of doom whilst the change to 'cares' has the effect of making Nelson's concern for Jamaica seem more personal, the implication being that if Jamaica were important to so great a man as Nelson, then it should be to the politicians and public at large. It should be noted that Nelson's 'fears' for Jamaica were primarily military – if Napoleon succeeded in capturing the island then Britain's resources would be diverted to the region leaving

England itself vulnerable to invasion. This indeed was Napoleon's intention when sending Villeneuve and the French fleet across the Atlantic in mid-1805.

Nelson states he would not see the 'just rights' of the West India possessions infringed. As noted above, Nelson was duty bound to protect those rights as an officer in the Royal Navy and by his oath of allegiance given to the King as a member of the House of Lords. In the NMRN letter the term 'just rights', however, is changed to 'interests', an amendment which clearly widens the scope of issues to be considered. It is not only the rights prescribed by law that are important, but wider interests, such as the economic and political effects and consequences of abolition (or so the anti-abolitionists wished to imply).

In the pressed letter, it has been seen that Nelson refers to the 'damnable cruel doctrine' of Wilberforce. If, as a result of this doctrine, the death of subjects in the colonies followed, Nelson would have perceived it as both damnable and cruel. The sentiment hints strongly at sympathy for all people in the colonies including enslaved people as well as the colonists and free black and people of colour. The anti-abolitionists, on the other hand, saw the end of the slave trade as disastrous to their interests, particularly economic, and hence changed the phrase 'damnable cruel doctrine' to 'damnable and cursed doctrine' in the doctored letter (a phrase embodying more than just a hint of bitterness). To the abolitionists it was not just the cruelty that would follow from abolition that concerned them (which was the scope of Nelson's concern) but rather the whole idea of abolition with its personal, economic and other consequences. After the abolition of the slave trade, Taylor wrote in similar terms: 'Cursed be the man who has bought in to this dilemma'.[20] This is a strong indication that Taylor was behind the alterations to Nelson's original letter.

Another significant change is that Nelson signs off the pressed letter as 'Your faithful and obliged friend and servant'. This is amended in the NMRN copy to 'Your faithful obliged servant'. The deletion of the word 'friend' removes any suggestion that this was intended to be a private and personal correspondence and not intended for public consumption or wide readership. It should be noted that, although Taylor had known Nelson for a number of years, they were neither close, nor regular correspondents, although they had been introduced by William Locker. Nelson's use of the familiar 'friend' seems designed to influence Taylor in the assistance that Nelson was seeking for Revd Dr Scott which was one of the prime purposes of the letter (see below).

The Planters' Friend?

Having realised that Nelson's letter had been forged it was possible to assess its contents in a new light and this leads to another potentially important discovery.

A substantial addition which appears at the end of the NMRN forged letter is in the form of a post-script. This states: 'The combined squadrons passed Antigua on the 8th. I am after them. Jamaica is safe on which I congratulate you most sincerely ...' (See Appendices 2 and 3). On 12th June 1805 Nelson had written to the Duke of Clarence, the future King William IV, to report the events in the Caribbean. He wrote 'The Combined Squadron passed to the leeward of Antigua on Saturday 8th.'[21]

He wrote in similar terms to William Marsden at the Admiralty: 'The French Fleet passed to leeward of Antigua on Saturday last ...'. It seems too much of a coincidence that the wording of the post-script added to the forged letter closely reflects Nelson's own words to the Duke of Clarence and William Marsden, when these words were not included in Nelson's original letter to Simon Taylor.

Marsden's views on the slave trade and slavery are not known but those of the Duke of Clarence were clear. The Duke held strong pro-slavery views and, from his very first speech in the House of Lords in 1792, supported the slave trade and slavery, based, as he stated, on his eye witness experiences in the West Indies whilst serving in the Navy. In that year, 1792, he was attending the House of Lords during a debate on the abolition of the slave trade when he rose, unprompted, and proclaimed that he considered the slave trade 'of the highest magnitude to the welfare and prosperity of the Kingdom'. He addressed the House in similar terms in 1793.

His experiences in the West Indies included attending balls, ceremonies and mixing with the luminaries of the planter class. It is unlikely that, in attending those functions, he would have seen, or been exposed to, the true circumstances of those slaves working in the plantation fields or sugar processing plants. Indeed, on a visit to Jamaica in 1789, it seemed to him that, in the fields and factories, the slaves seemed healthy and cheerful and, he concluded, they were probably happier there than in Africa. The degree to which such visits were stage managed by the planters can only be surmised but there is little doubt that they were keen to elicit and maintain his support, even suggesting that they would welcome his appointment as Governor of the island.

By way of contrast, the Duke of Clarence saw the abolitionists as hypocrites and fanatics, and his sentiments resonated with the planters such as Simon Taylor. He maintained his support for the system right through to the abolition of slavery itself, when there were even fears that, as King, he would not give Royal Assent to the Abolition of Slavery Act in 1834.

The Duke, as King, would become known as 'the planters' friend'.

It would appear, therefore, that the West Indian planters somehow had access to Nelson's correspondence to either the Duke or Marsden, although the circumstantial evidence points strongly towards the Duke, in light of his ties with the planters from his tour of duty in the West Indies and his vocal support of them. It is known that he also had links to the London West India Committee. Indeed he had attended one of its meetings in February 1805.[22]

The timing of access to the correspondence is also important. The Duke was in London in early 1806, and attended Nelson's funeral in January that year. It is known that the forgery was made early in 1806. Thus Simon Taylor must have had sight of, or at least a report of, the content of the letter to the Duke by that time, to enable the inclusion of the post-script, referencing Jamaica in the terms that it did, in the forgery.

The forged letter also provides some of the earliest evidence of a change in the tactics of the pro-slavery lobby to influence debates back in England. The planters' arguments, until the early 1790s, revolved around the inherent value of the slave trade, but shifted in that decade to the consequences of abolition on the well-being of the Empire, an approach encapsulated in the forged letter. The forged letter thus marks yet another significant step by the anti-abolitionists. That is, in the start of a 'dirty tricks' strategy in which it appears that the future king could have been complicit, inadvertently or otherwise. As part of that strategy the planters would seek to use Nelson's name and reputation in furtherance of their cause.

The later stages of that campaign would involve the continued use of Nelson's reputation, violence against ministers of the church on the island of Jamaica, and a heavily funded propaganda machine. There is no suggestion that the Duke encouraged the more violent aspects of the planters' activities but he did speak in favour of slavery on a number of occasions.

Fig 9: Prince William Henry

A second curiosity of the post-script is that Nelson, in writing to the Duke and to his agent and friend Alexander Davison, stated respectively '**I** … have saved these Colonies and 200 and upwards of sugar-laden ships ..' and '**I** have saved these Colonies and more than two hundred sail of sugar loaded ships'. It is more likely that, had Nelson himself added the post-script (which he did not), he would almost certainly have claimed credit for having saved Jamaica in terms such as '**I** have saved Jamaica' rather than 'Jamaica is safe on which I congratulate you', the term which appears in the forged version. In confirming the 'saving' of the colonies in his letters to

Davison and the Duke, Nelson was justifying his pursuit of the combined fleet in the absence of orders of the Admiralty, who, he thought, 'cannot be displeased'.

The 'congratulations' included in the NMRN forged post-script seeks to reinforce the impression, which the anti-abolitionists wished to create, that Jamaica was of personal importance to Nelson. Nelson had made that clear in the introduction to the letter: 'I was in a thousand fears for Jamaica ....', but even then that concern was framed by his understanding of French ambitions ('for that is a blow which Bonaparte would be happy to give us'). However, at the time he penned the letter to Simon Taylor, Nelson was convinced the combined enemy fleet was heading north, towards Antigua and away from Jamaica, which is a thousand miles to the west (see figure 3). So it proved and, in the event, Jamaica was never remotely under threat. It is known that Nelson put into St John's, Antigua on 12th June but the enemy fleet had passed by there several days before and Nelson chased them back to Europe. Consequently Nelson would never have needed to re-iterate the safety of Jamaica, as introduced in the forged post-script.

Given that the forgery was most likely penned in early 1806, the anti-abolitionists would have known the sequence of events associated with Nelson's pursuit of the combined enemy fleet in the Caribbean the previous summer, and that, in reality, Jamaica had never been threatened. Therefore, the purpose of the post-script, written at the behest of the Jamaican planters (and most probably by Simon Taylor, or at least under his direction), was to keep Jamaica in the public eye.

It is likely that all changes to the original letter by the anti-abolitionists were regarded as important, as otherwise they would have produced the original letter (or an accurate copy) without changes. (The NMRN forgery is reproduced in Appendix 2 and a full transcript of that letter is included as Appendix 3).

The forged copy of the original letter was sent to Taylor's friend, and fierce anti-abolitionist, William Cobbett, for publication in Cobbett's *Political Register.*[23]Given the content of the version which appeared in the *Political Register*, it is likely that Cobbett also had sight of the original letter. For example, the *Political Register* version of the letter retains amendments to the terminology such as 'interests' rather than 'just rights' but reverts back to 'fears' rather than 'cares'. It also retains the other amendments identified above, but adds one further significant change. In his original letter Nelson refers to the West India colonies forming a prominent and interesting part of the 'Public'. In the *Register* 'Public' is altered to 'Empire'. Again the intent is clear. The anti-abolitionists are preying on fears back in England, that any threat to the West Indies is a threat to British Empire. Another significant change is that the name 'Wilberforce' was removed from Cobbett's printed version of the letter, although this appears to be a convention of the period. The version of the letter which appeared in the *Political Register* is reproduced in Appendix 4.

Cobbett's version of the letter excluded Nelson's implied request to Taylor for his assistance in restoring an ecclesiastical living in Jamaica for the Reverend Dr Alexander Scott, then naval chaplain aboard HMS *Victory,* and a close friend of Nelson. Reverend Scott, born 1768, first met Nelson in 1793 when Nelson formed 'a proper estimate of his value'. In 1795 Scott became curate of St John's in Jamaica through the patronage of Sir Hyde Parker. When Sir Hyde Parker was relieved of his command and returned to England, Scott followed and joined him on the ship *Royal George.* Scott was suspended from his Jamaica living due to a prolonged absence and upon his return suffered a serious injury. Nelson frequently employed Scott's services and, for example, found Scott's linguistic skills of great use in the aftermath of the Battle of Copenhagen (see Chronology). Scott was unsuccessful in his attempt to recover his living which Nelson tried to help him secure in his letter to Simon Taylor. With Nelson's death, Scott's connection with the navy ceased.[24]

The NMRN forged copy letter was further annotated with a note that Scott had been killed at Trafalgar (see Appendices 2 and 3), which proves that the copy was made after news of the Battle reached Jamaica on 28thDecember 1805, but before it could be confirmed that it was Nelson's secretary John Scott, and not his chaplain Alexander Scott, who had been killed.

Nelson and the Duke of Clarence

Prince William Henry had joined the Navy as a midshipman in June 1779 at the age of 13, his first ship being the *Prince George.*

Nelson and the Prince first met in New York in 1782, during the American War of Independence. Nelson had arrived in the *Albemarle* from Quebec and the Prince thought he was the 'merest boy' of a captain he ever met. Nelson thought the Prince would make a good sailor.

In early 1783, just prior to the peace of Amiens, Nelson was seeking the French in the West Indies when the Prince arrived in Jamaica under the guidance of Lord Hood. The Council of Jamaica was pleased by the prince's presence and it was during this visit that Lord Hood placed him under the care and direction of Nelson. Nelson was eight years the Prince's senior and a long lasting friendship developed. By 1786 the prince was promoted to Captain and had established a reputation as a strong disciplinarian.

Again in the West Indies the Prince found himself under Nelson's command and their friendship strengthened, with Prince William insisting on giving away Fanny at her wedding with Nelson in 1787. The Prince supported Nelson over his implementation of the Navigation Acts and his presence ashore ensured that Nelson was not totally ostracised by the colonial society of the islands.

It clearly suited Nelson to have royal connections in advancing his career, particularly after the death of his only major sponsor, his uncle Maurice Suckling. It also clearly benefited the Duke to have associated with Nelson at a time when his reputation and accolades far exceeded those that even a king might expect. There is no doubt that the Duke developed a strong love for the navy and had an enduring friendship with Nelson. But, despite that, there is no evidence, either reported or in writing, that they shared similar views on the issue of the slave trade or slavery. It is probable, as Pocock put it, they were more likely to have been taxed by 'sailors' politics'.

A Second Discovery

Since the discovery of the forged (NMRN) version of the Nelson-Taylor letter in 2018 a further forged version of the letter has been come to light. It was put up for auction in 2018 and again its importance only realised latterly. The destiny of this version of the letter is unknown but a 'screen shot' of the letter was taken from the auction catalogue and this is reproduced in Appendix 5 with a transcript of this forgery in Appendix 6. This version of the Nelson-Taylor letter is in a different handwriting to that of the NMRN version, now kept in Portsmouth. It was posted to a Duncan Campbell, whose address appears on the letter, and who was residing in Buxton at the time.

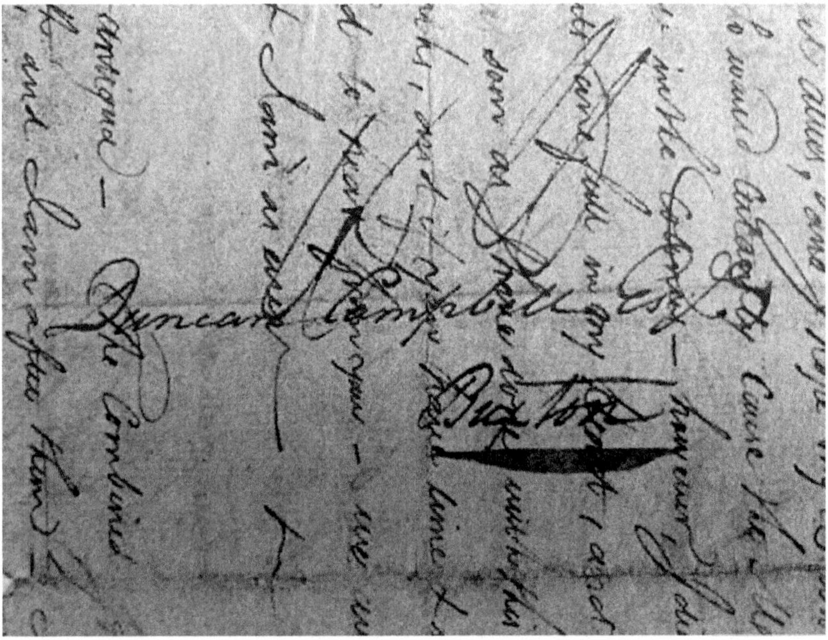

Fig 10: Address detail from the Campbell letter (see also Appendix 5)

The author of this copy of the letter is unknown. It is known that a Campbell family were significant plantation and slave holders in the Black River area of Jamaica and they, and others of this surname, were beneficiaries of the compensation scheme after the abolition of slavery in 1834. It is not clear whether the Duncan Campbell to whom the letter was addressed was the one from a slave owning family or the Duncan Campbell who was elected to Parliament in 1809 as a Whig. However, the Campbell to whom the letter was sent was clearly a supporter of slavery (why else would the letter have been sent to him?).

The importance of this version of the letter (hereinafter referred to as the Campbell letter) is that it clearly demonstrates that the planters were acting in a co-ordinated way in seeking to use Nelson's private correspondence and reputation to influence the debate on the abolition of the slave trade. It too is a corrupted version of the original letter and retains wording such as 'Empire' in place of 'Public' and 'damnable and cursed doctrine of Wilberforce' found in the earlier NMRN letter. It also contains a number of other 'editorial' changes which are apparent when it is compared to the pressed letter and the NMRN forgery.

Of further importance is that this version of the letter confirms that copies of the forged letter were in wide circulation in early 1807. The Campbell letter excludes the plea to assist the Revd Scott in securing an ecclesiastical living on Jamaica and clearly shows that the planters were working in concert in using Nelson's letter and posthumous reputation for their own ends. Indeed this strategy can be seen as part of a wide-reaching, sophisticated, often violent and well-organised campaign that would run through the abolition of the slave trade and abolition of slavery campaigns, in which the pro-slavery lobby invested considerable time, effort and finance.[25]

But where was this forgery made? It can reasonably be assumed that the NMRN forgery was made in Jamaica. After all, that is where the original letter was sent with its seal, which was re-used in the forgery. However, the Campbell forgery has no (recoverable) seal but it does have a 'postmark'. Advice from the Royal Philatelic Society London confirms that the 'postmark' is a UK mark. Further enquiries were made of the British Postmark Society. They concluded the postmark would have been applied at the General Post Office in the City of London (which was situated in Lombard Street) in 1806, thus ruling out the possibility that the letter was a later forgery. Postmarks, or 'stamps' of the period, show the year of 'franking' in 2 or 3 figures –

hence 806 for the year 1806. The stamp is clearly visible on the reproduction of the letter in Appendix 5. All this confirms the passage of the letter through London, which was probably where the letter originated when it was copied from the Simon Taylor (NMRN) forgery. This supports the theory of a wide-spread attempt by the planters and their representatives in Britain to influence the outcome of the debates in Parliament by using Nelson's reputation.

The Campbell forgery is also interesting in that there are several markings in pencil on the letter. These appear to be of twentieth century origin. At the top of the letter these markings note that this is a 'contemporary copy' (of Nelson's original letter) made 'by Nelson's Secretary'. It is not known precisely when these notes were added but, as evidenced above, this copy could not have been made by Nelson's secretary, John Scott, as he had been killed on HMS *Victory* at Trafalgar in October 1805 before changes to the original letter were made in 1806.

A further pencil note at the bottom of the letter is intriguing, however. It suggests that this copy of the letter was sent to the Right Honourable Second Earl Camden, Sir John Jeffreys Pratt. Sir John Pratt (1759-1840) was the Secretary of State for War and the Colonies in Pitt's government from 1804-5. He was also Lord President of the Council from 1807 to 1812, hence a most important, senior and influential member of the government. It would come as no surprise, therefore, that the anti-abolitionists would seek his support, although this note is unverified.

The anti-abolitionists clearly went to a great deal of trouble to embroil Nelson on their side of the slave trade debates. However, they could not be confident that he supported their views. He was certainly conservative in his outlook but his letter to Simon Taylor did not give the anti-abolitionists the comfort or support they were seeking. We can assume that Nelson was aware of how the reader, Simon Taylor, would receive his letter. It was, after all, a personal and private letter. The letter would have been framed by Nelson in the knowledge as to how it would have been received, read and interpreted by Taylor.

Fig 11: Sir John Jeffreys Pratt.

So, in stating that he did not 'intend to have gone so far' in the sentiments he expressed in the letter, he would have known that he did not go far enough in the eyes of Simon Taylor and his pro-slavery friends. He fell short of expressing support for either the slave trade or slavery – his letter was carefully crafted to demonstrate his support for the colonial system. The anti-abolitionists saw, that in its original form, the letter would not serve their purpose. Nelson's death at Trafalgar, and his heroic status, presented the anti-abolitionists with the unexpected opportunity to heavily doctor the letter in the knowledge that Nelson would not be there to explain precisely what he meant in the letter, or contradict the content of the forger(ies).

A further question arises. Why did the anti-abolitionists not make more significant changes to the letter? They certainly changed key words in the letter to reinforce their interests but there was clearly a danger in going too far. Those who knew Nelson best would almost certainly have jumped to his defence if sentiments were ascribed to him that he did not hold. Those colleagues would have included his close friend Hercules Ross and his protégé William Layman, as well as those officers, such as Admiral Collingwood and Captain Hardy, with whom he spent a considerable amount of time. The recent discovery of the forgeries does not, of course, put Nelson into the abolitionist camp but they do show that he was not in the pro-slavery camp, as has been alleged. The wording of his original letter displays his awareness of the wider debate and understanding of the sensitivities involved if a senior officer of the Royal Navy became embroiled in that debate. That there was a concerted effort in circulating these forgeries and publicising their content is reinforced by a further reference to the letter in the case of Sir Home Popham. In that instance the reason for referring to the letter is one other than the slave trade.

Sir Home Riggs Popham (1762-1820)

Sir Home Riggs Popham was a colourful and controversial figure who joined the navy as an able seaman in 1778, after abandoning his education at Trinity College, Cambridge, where he was enrolled after attending Westminster School.

Popham is best remembered for creating the system of naval signalling which was used by Nelson at Trafalgar ('England Expects That Every Man Will Do his Duty'). That system was designed in about 1800 and was formally adopted by the Admiralty in 1812. Popham served under Admiral George Rodney during the American War of Independence when he was captured by the French in 1781. After his release he gained a reputation as an excellent hydrographer, following a survey of the coast of south-west Africa in 1786. In 1787 he faced a period 'on the beach' and, on gaining leave from the Admiralty, he bought his first ship and sailed for India as a trader. His commercial activities came under close scrutiny and Popham was suspected of trading in contravention of the East India Company's charter. As a result he suffered considerable losses and, having failed to renew his leave, was also temporarily struck off the Royal Navy's lieutenants' register.

Upon re-instatement in 1793 Popham was appointed agent for the Transports at Ostend during the campaign of the Duke of York in Flanders, being responsible for the evacuation of allied forces in 1795. Further adventures and controversies followed in the Helder peninsula and with Abercromby in Egypt.

Most significantly Popham was appointed commodore of HMS *Diadem,* leading an expedition to recover the Cape of Good Hope, then occupied by the Dutch, in 1805. The operation, in which Popham was supported by General Sir David Baird, was a great success and the Dutch surrendered the colony. Buoyed by this success Popham decided to attack Buenos Aires on the River Plate, an act which he assumed would receive political support. Buenos Aires was, at the time, under Spanish control and the Spanish were allies of the French in the war against Britain. On 25th June 1806, a force of some 1,635 men under Brigadier General Beresford landed near Buenos Aires and met with little resistance from the Spanish occupiers who surrendered on 2nd July. An excited Popham wrote an open letter to traders in England advising them of a new market for their goods. However a Spanish force recovered the city on August 10th capturing Beresford and his men. Popham blockaded the river and awaited reinforcements. When these arrived they carried orders for Popham to return to England. Upon arrival Popham was arrested pending a court martial in which he was charged, inter alia, with having invaded Argentina 'without direction or authority'.

Popham was tried in Portsmouth in March 1807. In his defence Popham cited a number of instances where officers had conducted attacks 'without orders' – Parker and Dalling against the Spanish settlement at Omaoh; Lord Hood entering Toulon in 1795; Lord St Vincent sending 'the heroic Nelson' to attack Tenerife in 1797. He then stated: 'But let the court particularly look at the letter recently published by that illustrious officer, Lord Nelson, to Simon Taylor, of

Jamaica, relative to his discretion in going from the Mediterranean to the West Indies'.[26]

In his letter Nelson stated '...I flew to the West Indies without any orders, but I think the Ministry cannot be displeased.' It was this action upon which Popham relied in his defence. (It will be recalled that Nelson was keen to justify this action and consistently referred, in correspondence, to his having saved the colonies and upwards of 200 sugar ships). Clearly Nelson's letter, or more specifically the corrupted version of it, was in circulation, to be called upon by Popham in March 1807. It was likely that Popham was referring to the version of the letter published in the *Political Register* in February 1807. Popham was subsequently found guilty and severely reprimanded although this seems not to have done his later career any harm. He was appointed Captain of the Fleet for the second battle of Copenhagen (16th August -7th September 1807) and eventually became Commander-in-Chief of Jamaica 1817-20. Sir Home Popham died in 1820 and is buried in the churchyard of St Michael and All Angels at Sunninghill in Berkshire, close to his home, now demolished.

Fig 12: Sir Home Riggs Popham.

8

FORGERIES COMPOUNDED

As previously noted, versions of Nelson's letter to Taylor have appeared in Clarke and McArthur's *The Life and Services of Admiral Lord Nelson,* second edition 1840 (it did not appear in the first edition of 1809), in Nicolas *The Dispatches and Letters of Vice Admiral Lord Viscount Nelson* (first published between 1844 and 1846), and in the *Naval Miscellany*(1901). None of these is an accurate representation or transcript of the original letter although, together with the version which appeared in the *Political Register,* they appear to be the only versions relied on by historians and past biographers of Nelson, subject to one unusual exception which is examined below.[27] All copies of the letter are reproduced in Appendices 1-9.

The analysis above of certain key phrases in the original letter and subsequent versions of the letter shows how they were changed, or even omitted, as they have been reproduced over the past two hundred years or so. Those phrases are 'thousand fears'; 'serve the Public'; 'just rights'; damnable cruel doctrine'; and Nelson's request about the Revd Dr Scott. Also included is the addition by the abolitionists about the safety of Jamaica. Key features of the letters are summarised in the table below.

There are a number of conclusions to be drawn from the Table. The first is that Nelson's original letter to Simon Taylor was certainly and significantly altered, after Nelson's death, for publication and to influence the debate on the abolition of the slave trade. Secondly, at least one other version of the letter, the Campbell version, was in circulation and it is highly likely that others were too. Thirdly, other versions of the letter, relying on the forged copies, have been published at various times and subsequently relied upon by historians when considering the question of Nelson, race and the slave trade. Fourthly, in 1806-7, the West Indian 'interest' ramped up the scare-mongering relating to the impacts of abolition on the Empire and targeted William Wilberforce as a purveyor of a 'damnable and cursed doctrine' (unlike Nelson who, for reasons explained earlier, saw it as a 'damnable cruel doctrine').

COMPARATIVE ASSESSMENT OF KEY FEATURES OF PRESSED LETTER AND SUBSEQUENT VERSIONS

Pressed Letter 1805 (Nelson)	**Thousand Fears**	**Serve the Public**	**Just Rights**	**Damnable Cruel Doctrine**	**Rev.Dr Scott Request**	
Taylor Forgery 1806 NMRN	Thousand Cares	Serve the Public	Interest	Damnable and Cursed Doctrine	Rev.Scott Request	Jamaica is safe
Campbell Forgery 1806	Thousand Fears	Serve the Empire	Interest	Damnable and Cursed Doctrine		Jamaica is safe
Political Register 1807	Thousand Fears	Serve the Empire	Interest	Damnable and Cursed Doctrine		Jamaica is safe
Clark and McArthur 1840	Thousand Fears	Serve the Public Weal	Just Rights			
Nicolas 1844-46	Thousand Fears	Serve the Public Weal	Just Rights			
Naval Miscellany 1901	Thousand Cares	Serve the Public	Interest	Damnable and Cursed Doctrine	Rev.Scott Request	Jamaica is safe

Fifthly, after the NMRN version of the letter, the anti-abolitionists preferred the more doom laden term 'fears' to 'cares', which implied wider ramifications for the Empire. Sixthly, most versions exclude its real purpose which was that of securing employment for the Reverend Scott. Finally, none of the versions accurately reflects the original letter. It would appear that Laughton, in *The Naval Miscellany* 1901, had access to the NMRN forged version of the letter as he includes the term 'thousand cares' and the Revd Dr Scott 'request' which only appear together in that version.

It is also interesting to note that the letter did not feature in the first edition of Clarke and McArthur's work in 1809. Perhaps the subject matter was deemed too sensitive at the time. The version which appeared in the 1840 reprint, a number of years after the abolition of slavery, seems to be an amalgam of various sources including, intriguingly, the original letter. It includes, for example, the term 'just rights' which hitherto had only appeared in Nelson's original.

The difficulty of relying on the printed sources of Nelson's letters has already been alluded to and, as Colling notes,

'*Primary sources are the real treasure of historians'*.[28]

He concludes that there is much work to be done over the next few years to ensure that Nelson's true written words are recorded for posterity and, it might be added, as an invaluable source of information for historians.

Of course, the above analysis of Nelson's letter involves some speculation. In speculating, regard has been had to the primacy of the source material – whilst seeking to understand the context within which it was written and Nelson's views which shaped it.

The timing of events is also significant. Lord Grenville succeeded Pitt as Prime Minister upon the latter's death in 1806. It was Grenville who, together with Pitt, had first proposed the idea of abolition to Wilberforce. During the parliamentary recess of 1806 Grenville conceived the idea of taking the bill for the abolition of the slave trade to the Lords first, to reduce the opportunity for the anti-abolitionists to drag out proceedings – if time became tight the bill could be discussed in the Commons at the same time. Thus the Act for the Abolition of the Slave Trade had its first reading in the House of Lords in January 1807. The Bill was passed at its second reading on 5th February 1807 by 100 votes to 34 and was, after a third reading on 10th February, returned to the Commons. On 21st February 1807 Cobbett's *Political Register* published the doctored copy of the Nelson-Taylor letter, two days before the Bill was debated in the Commons, presumably in a last-ditch effort to use Nelson's considerable posthumous reputation to influence the outcome of the vote. A reference was also made to the letter in the *Annual Register* for February 1807. (However, the 1807 *Annual Register* was not published until 1809 and could not have affected the passage of the Act). The Bill was approved by the Commons, receiving Royal Assent on 25th March 1807.

A timeline showing the dates of publication and use of various versions of the letter in the progress of the Act for the Abolition of the Slave Trade, and subsequently, is shown in Appendix 10.

A further curiosity is the appearance, some 25 years after the death of Nelson, of another version of the forged letters. This appeared in a strange and fascinating little pamphlet entitled *'False Sanctity'*.

False Sanctity[29]

In 1831 Roake and Verity, publishers in London, issued a booklet entitled *'False Sanctity (Versified) or The Modern Tartuffes: To My Country'*. This publication is intriguing as it contains yet another version of (an extract) of the Nelson-Taylor letter.

In summary the booklet is a versified report of an imagined meeting of the London Anti-Slavery Society. It is in the form of a play reporting on the meeting. The meeting is chaired by Mr B_x_n, a thinly disguised reference to Thomas Buxton, a well-known abolitionist. In addressing the meeting Mr Buxton says (original spelling and punctuation maintained):

"Who cares what *fifty Officers* have stated,
Who cares for all that *Rodney* has related?
Does not the public, trust to you, and me
More than to *Nelson*, or *His M______y?*
Who does not think the *first* had lost his wits,
When he pronounc'd us, *knaves,* and *hypocrites?*
And said, that though the *Planter's friend* was he,
He thought his *berth in Heav'n,* as *high* might be,
As that of *W__b___ce* or *Z_ch_ry**"

The footnote to this verse reads:

**Lord Nelson's letter to a friend in Jamaica, dated Victory 1803* – "I have ever been, and shall be, a firm friend to our present Colonial system: I was bred, as you know, in the good old school, and taught the value of our West India possessions, and neither in the field , nor in the Senate, shall their just rights be infringed, while I have an arm to fight in their defence, or a tongue to launch my voice against the damnable and cruel doctrine of W__B____ce, and his hypocritical allies; and I hope my berth in heaven will be as exalted as his, who would certainly cause the murder of all our friends and fellow subjects in the colonies".

False Sanctity, author unknown, is a homage to the French playwright Moliere's play *Tartuffe* (known in English as 'The Impostor') first performed in 1664, and which was written in twelve syllable lines of rhyming couplets. The name of the chief character of Moliere's play, 'Tartuffe', became a term used to describe a hypocrite who feigns virtue, especially religious virtue. *False Sanctity* is a satirical play that features a number of prominent abolitionists such as Thomas Buxton, Zachary McCauley and George Stephen – the modern Tartuffes of the title.

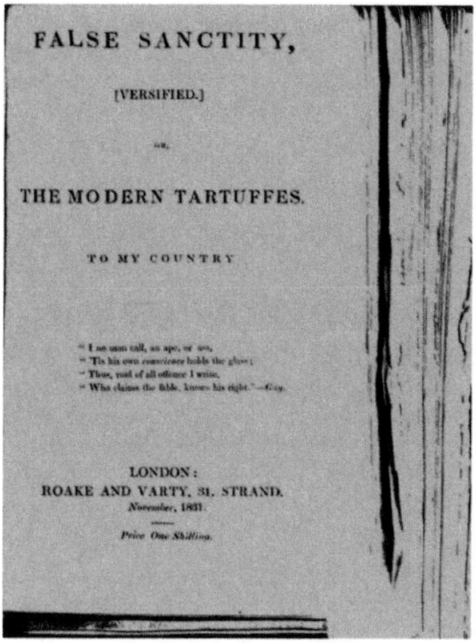

FALSE SANCTITY,

[VERSIFIED.]

OR,

THE MODERN TARTUFFES.

TO MY COUNTRY

"I no man call, an ape, or ass,
"'Tis his own *conscience* holds the glass;
"Thus, void of all offence I write,
"Who claims the fable, knows his right."—*Gay.*

LONDON:
ROAKE AND VARTY, 31, STRAND.
November, 1831.

Price One Shilling.

Fig. 13: False Sanctity 1831.

A careful reading of the 'play' shows that this is a piece of anti-abolitionist propaganda. It was produced at a period when the Whigs had just taken control of Parliament and were confident of pushing through reforming legislation followed by a thrust to abolish slavery (which they succeeded in doing in 1834). In the play the name given to abolitionists is the 'Anti-Slavery Society', whose members are referred by the acronym ASSes. In the play, Mr Buxton believes every village should have one! He says '*..it's well known abbreviation can scarcely need this prosing explanation'!*

There are a number of other heavily sarcastic references. Of Wilberforce Buxton says:

"Great *W__b___ce,* now aged, bent and hoary,
In privacy, enjoys his well-earned glory:
This *title* is his due (the world confesses)
FATHER, *of all the great A double S es!!"*

Later in the play it is stated:

" 'Tis *(entre nous)* a grievous thing,
That we may not elect a K__g,
Who'd be the Planter's *enemy;*
(Unlike His present M_____y)
" Yet could we choose – 'tis very plain,
A royal W_ll__m, still should reign!!"

This latter passage pours scorn on Wilberforce, suggesting the abolitionists would propose him to be King if they had the choice, unlike the planter's friend, His Majesty King William IV.

Of particular significance is the footnote with its reference to Nelson, which quotes an extract from the Nelson-Taylor letter. There are a number of differences between this quote and the contents of the pressed letter. First the letter is seemingly dated 1803 when it is known that it was written in June 1805. However, only Taylor and a limited number of his allies knew that the letter seemingly responded to Taylor's letter to Nelson of October 1802. Of course the extract of the letter included in the play conveniently omits the first part of the letter which deals with Nelson's pursuit of the French in June 1805 and which would give the lie to the seemingly timely reply by Nelson to Taylor's 1802 letter.

Secondly, Nelson says in the original letter he was 'taught **to appreciate** the value of our West India possessions'. The omission of the phrase 'to appreciate' makes the value of the colonies to Nelson seem absolute to the reader. Indeed, the anti-abolitionists put the economic and political value of the colonies centrally in their arguments in debates on abolition of the slave trade in 1807 and in the subsequent debates on the abolition of slavery itself. Finally Nelson refers to 'the damnable cruel doctrine' (of Wilberforce) not 'the damnable **and** cruel doctrine'. On the face of it this does not seem significant but when it is remembered that the word 'cruel' did not appear in any of the forged versions of the letter or the version of the letter printed in Cobbett's Political Register in 1807, only the anti-abolitionists could have known of Nelson's use of this word. This is more evidence that the forged documents were authored by the pro-slavery lobby.

Thus the West Indian planters were still seeking to use Nelson's reputation (he had been elevated to almost god-like status in the public mind) some 26 years after his death. In the passage referring to Nelson above they pose the question, in a tone of heavy irony, 'doesn't the public trust you and me' (the Asses!) 'rather than Nelson or his Majesty?'. Further, again with irony, they ask 'hadn't Nelson lost his senses when he accused Wilberforce and his allies of being hypocritical' and that his berth in heaven would be as exalted as Wilberforce's and Zachary McCauley's? (Nelson's view of Wilberforce as a 'hypocrite' is explained above). The implication is that the public should support Nelson, albeit on the basis of the letter written and forged long ago, and the King, rather than trust the abolitionists – indeed they would be foolish to trust the ASSes! The forged Nelson-Taylor letter resonates throughout the history of the battles between the pro-slavery lobby and the abolitionists right through until the abolition of slavery in 1834, and continues to cast a shadow even today.

It is interesting to note that the use of the forged versions of Nelson's letter continues today. In his excellent book *The Interest: How the British Establishment Resisted the Abolition of Slavery* the author Michael Taylor quotes the letter and his source – *The Dispatches and Letters of Vice Admiral Lord Viscount Nelson* edited by Sir Nicholas Harris Nicolas. However the version reproduced in Taylor's book does not match that in Nicolas. The Nicolas version contains no reference to Wilberforce but the quote in Taylor's book (p71) does, and includes the phrase 'damnable and cruel doctrine', which only appears in '*False Sanctity*!'(Nelson used a similar term: 'damnable cruel doctrine'). This is suggestive that even in 1831 (the publication year of *False Sanctity!*) the anti-abolitionists may have retained the original version of Nelson's letter to Taylor, with its reference to 'cruel doctrine'. (see Table p94 above).

An Unattributed Reference

In his book, *'Bury the Chains: The British Struggle to Abolish Slavery'*, Adam Hochschild maintains that war fever (i.e. the war with France) wrapped slavery tightly in the British flag. In quoting from (a version of) the Nelson-Taylor letter he states that Nelson declared that he would battle any threat to the West India possessions '…while I have an arm to fight in their defence, or a tongue to launch my voice against the damnable doctrine of Wilberforce and his hypocritical allies'. Although in quotation marks there is no attribution of the source. The term 'damnable doctrine' does not appear in any other of the versions of the letter discovered in the course of this study and may well be an 'editorial' corruption, unless there is another version of the letter in an, as yet, unidentified source.

9

NELSON AND Lt. LAYMAN[30]

It has been noted on several occasions in this study that Nelson supported the idea of paid labour in the West Indies colonies. One such idea was mooted by Lieutenant Layman RN, who was well known to Nelson.
William Layman (1768-1826) entered the Royal Navy in 1782 and in about 1788 he joined the merchant service, employed in the East India and China regions. He re-joined the Navy in 1800 having approached Nelson to support his ambitions. Layman was committed to serving with Nelson and, upon passing his Lieutenant's exam, eventually joined Nelson on HMS *St George*, in Torbay, in 1801.
Layman distinguished himself in the Baltic Campaign at the Battle of Copenhagen and was held in high regard by Nelson who gave him the following testimonial:

'My dear Sir,– I have been favored with your letter, requesting I would state the nature of the services you had been employed in from the St. George.
That you were always ready to go on every service I am sure; for the only favor you ever asked of me was, to be sent on all services of danger and difficulties, and I always understood you acquitted yourself as an able officer and seaman. You were in the Isis at the battle of Copenhagen, and Captain Walker gave me a high character of the conduct of the officers and men of the St. George. Believe me to be fully sensible of all your merits; and I have no scruple in saying, that if your interest does not get you promoted, at any future time when I may be employed, I shall be happy in receiving you; for I am your sincere friend.
Nelson & Bronte'

On 25th May 1802 the Peace of Amiens was concluded between Britain and France. The British conceded several of their Caribbean gains but retained Trinidad. Napoleon re-asserted French claims to Saint-Domingue in May and declared slavery officially re-instated on that island. On 27th May George Canning brought forward a motion in the Commons aiming to outlaw slave plantations on Trinidad. (Wilberforce decided at this stage to let Canning run his idea and delayed bringing forward a new abolition bill). Canning argued that Trinidad could become a new concept in the Caribbean: *'a bloodless, guiltless colony.'* [31] In the event, Addington, the Prime Minister since Pitt's resignation in February 1801, advised that Canning's motion was not needed, as Trinidad was currently being surveyed and would be discussed by Parliament the following year.

During the Peace of Amiens Lieutenant Layman occupied his time and maintained his profile by submitting several proposals to the Government based on his experiences in the Far East. Of particular interest was his proposal in response to the notice given in the House of Commons by George Canning. Layman was of the view that slavery was not only morally repugnant but also ineffective. He suggested, therefore, the replacement of slave labour with paid Chinese labourers, whom he regarded as both skilful and productive. With appropriate support the Chinese might set an example to existing slaves who might become free labourers with a means of supporting themselves.

Layman's proposals were considered by the Colonial office and eventually made their way to Samuel Hood, a Commissioner for Trinidad. Layman was invited to present his proposals to senior members of the Commission.

In May 1803 the British Government declared war on France, the Peace of Amiens now appearing more of a truce between two exhausted nations. Wilberforce, not for the first time, opposed the declaration. Such a stance would not have endeared him to Nelson.

After the Commission for Trinidad closed down, and Layman had sailed for the Mediterranean in 1803, a project was undertaken in the same year, involving the taking of some 200 Chinese workers to Trinidad. Badly managed, the project failed. Layman was surprised to hear about the project and that several people claimed that the (Layman) idea was theirs, or had put forward similar proposals. This prompted Layman to write to Samuel Hood who confirmed that Layman was indeed the originator of the scheme, in the following terms:[32]

"H.M.S. Centaur, Sept 3d, 1806.

'Sir,– I have to acknowledge the receipt of your letter, on the subject of a plan you submitted to Government in 1802, for the cultivation of

Trinidad, which was referred by the Secretary of State to the Commissioners for that island, and in consequence of which you met us by appointment at the Treasury, and were informed by the Right Hon. John Sullivan, then Under Secretary of State, that the execution of the measure only waited an official report of the Commissioners. The termination of the commission, owing to the disagreement between Colonels Fullerton and Picton, certainly prevented the report; and as you state it is unknown to his Majesty's present Ministers in whom the idea first originated, I have great pleasure in telling you, I always understood the plan of introducing Chinese into the West Indies was first suggested by you, whilst I was one of the said Commissioners; and I must. Sir, do you the justice to say, I never heard of any other person having proposed such a measure. Yours, &c.

(Signed) SAMUEL HOOD'

Layman also received a further letter on the subject from the then Secretary to the Treasury and later Chancellor of the Exchequer, Nicholas Vansittart. That letter was dated 11th December 1806. It reads:

'*Sir*

I have been favoured with your letter of yesterday, and beg leave to state in answer, that I have no difficulty in confirming the fact of your having made the first proposition to government which came within my knowledge, for conveying Chinese labourers to the West Indies. You were introduced to me as you state, by Mr Wilson, ***and I believe by a letter from Lord Nelson*** *(though I am not sure of the time I received it); and the proposition seemed to me to be so deserving of attention that I immediately mentioned it to Mr Sullivan...'* (author's emphasis).[33]

These letters were presented to the committee of the House of Commons who were 'fully impressed with the important advantages which might, under proper arrangements, be expected to result to the West India Islands, from the introduction of a class of free people, so distinguished by their orderly and industrious habits'.[34]

It is clear that Nelson saw fit to introduce Layman and his proposal to a key member of the government, Nicholas Vansittart, whom Nelson regarded as a friend and one who would always be welcome at his and Emma's home in Merton. Layman was known to have visited Nelson at Merton during his period there during the peace in 1802 and would, no doubt, have discussed his ideas with him. The measured scheme suggested by Layman was likely to have appealed to Nelson, with its step by step approach to replacing slavery with paid labour – it should be noted that the end objective of the proposal was the replacement of slavery, not just the need to abolish the slave trade. Nelson clearly felt the proposal had merit and supported it, otherwise he would not have exposed a junior officer, whom he rated very highly, to high ranking members of the government, on such a high profile and controversial issue. It is clear from the wording of Vansittart's letter that Nelson's introduction of Layman was in the context of Layman's proposals for the West Indies.

Having received the letters of endorsement from Hood and Vansittart and keen to establish his claim to the idea, in 1807 Layman felt it necessary to publish his proposal for a wider audience. Entitled '*Outline of a Plan for the Cultivation, Security and Defence of the British West Indies: Being the Original Suggestion for Providing an Effectual Substitute for the African Slave and Preventing the Dependance of Those Colonies on America for Supplies'*. In the Introduction to the text he describes the advent of his proposals and the support they received from members of the (government's) administration.

Nelson's support for Layman's ideas are a strong indication that he was not a fervent supporter of the slave trade or slavery but saw Layman's propositions as a way of sustaining the Colonies. It should be noted that neither William Pitt, when Prime Minister, nor William Wilberforce, were advocating the abandonment of the colonies. They were trying to find a way of securing their future without reliance on the slave trade or slavery. As alluded to earlier, Pitt and Wilberforce were able to separate the colonies from slavery (which many modern commentators seem to be unable to recognise) and there is no reason to suppose that Nelson could and did not do the same.

Layman had a colourful career, bringing forward several radical ideas for the betterment of the Navy and survived several courts martial. He sadly took his own life on 22nd May 1826, the navy having lost a most innovative and creative asset.

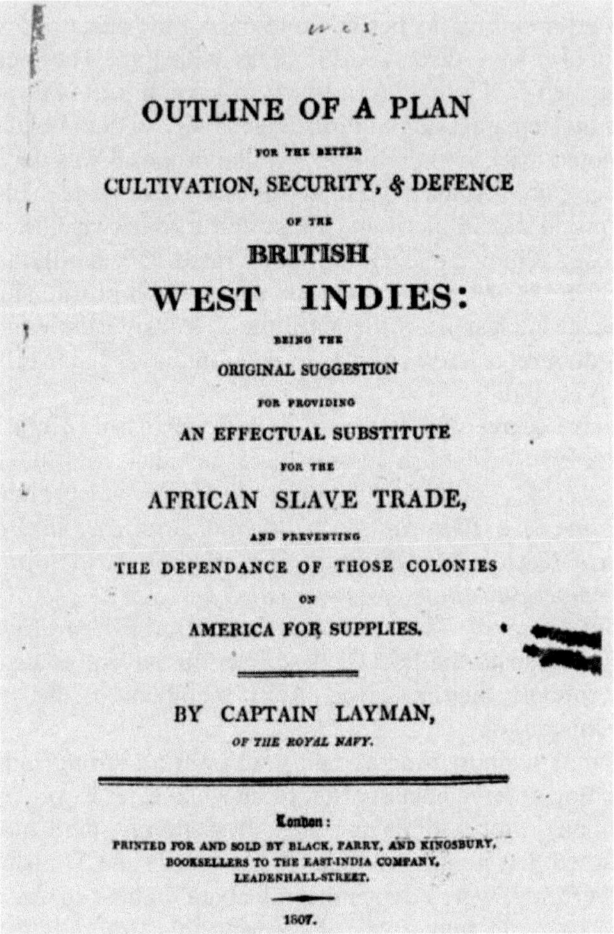

OUTLINE OF A PLAN

FOR THE BETTER

CULTIVATION, SECURITY, & DEFENCE

OF THE

BRITISH

WEST INDIES:

BEING THE

ORIGINAL SUGGESTION

FOR PROVIDING

AN EFFECTUAL SUBSTITUTE

FOR THE

AFRICAN SLAVE TRADE,

AND PREVENTING

THE DEPENDANCE OF THOSE COLONIES

ON

AMERICA FOR SUPPLIES.

BY CAPTAIN LAYMAN,

OF THE ROYAL NAVY.

London:

PRINTED FOR AND SOLD BY BLACK, PARRY, AND KINGSBURY,
BOOKSELLERS TO THE EAST-INDIA COMPANY,
LEADENHALL-STREET.

1807.

Fig.14: The Layman Plan.

10

A REPUTATION RESTORED?

That slavery and the slave trade underpinned the colonial system was, of course, known to Nelson. However, that system existed before he was born and existed when he joined the Navy, and existed after his death. It was the context within which he grew up, lived and operated. There is no evidence that Nelson supported slavery as either an economic, philosophical or social concept: it was a system that existed and was part of the context within which he operated as a professional naval officer.

His response when faced with specific issues touching on the subject was generally humane and pragmatic. For example:

- Any West Indian slaves escaping to a Navy ship were signed on, paid and afforded the same treatment as other crew members. At the end of their service they were discharged as free men.[35]
- In 1799 Nelson intervened to secure the release of 24 North African slaves being held in Portuguese galleys off Palermo.[36]
- Nelson intervened seeking to secure the release of slaves off North Africa, caught up in the Barbary slave trade.
- In 1802 when it was proposed by Lt Layman that plantation slaves in Trinidad should be replaced by free industrious Chinese labourers, Nelson supported the idea and introduced Layman to members of the government to promote his ideas.
- In 1803 Nelson rescued the black Haitian General, Joseph Chretien, and his servant from the French. They asked if they could serve with Nelson and Nelson recommended that they be paid until they could be discharged and granted passage to Jamaica. The General's mission was to end slavery, a fact of which Nelson was well aware. The General and his servant were well treated and paid.[37]
- Nelson treated all men of different ethnicities with respect as evidenced by the personal relationships set out in Section 3 above.

These are not the actions of someone who was avidly pro-slavery or racist in the modern sense. It was entirely consistent for Nelson to support the colonial system, as an officer of an executive arm of the state - the Royal Navy - with its dependence on the slave trade, but still not be pro-slavery or a 'white supremacist' as he has been labelled. This was a conclusion reached by the eminent Nelson historian, Dr Colin White in 2007. In the *Trafalgar Chronicle* 2007, the bicentenary year of the Act to abolish the Slave Trade, the Editor sought a note to substantiate Nelson's attitude to towards the system of slavery. The Note saw the difficulties of relying upon the versions of the Nelson-Taylor letter published in both Nicolas and Clarke and McArthur. With the question being 'of prime importance' the Editor appealed to Dr White, then Director of the Royal Naval Museum in Portsmouth, for clarification. Dr White responded as follows:

'I am afraid the answer is that Nelson most definitely did write the words attributed to him. Clarke and McArthur (who saw the original) did their usual trick of editing out potentially embarrassing or 'sensitive' material and Nicolas (who did not see the original) simply copied from C&M. I have not seen the original, and do not know where it is, but I have seen the 'pressed copy' in one of the British Library volumes I discovered (BL Add MS 34959) and there can be no doubt about it – the passage about 'Wilberforce and his hypocritical allies' is definitely there. You will remember that the pressed copies are direct impressions of the originals and so I have seen the words in Nelson's own handwriting. If you want to see the full text of the letter, it was printed by Laughton in his Naval Miscellany. Infuriatingly, Laughton – as so often – does not give a reference for the letter, so we do not know if he was working from an original, or where he found it. I think we have to confront this issue head on. Nelson, as he says, was 'bred in the good old school' and so, like very many of his contemporaries, he was exceedingly worried about Wilberforce and his campaign against slavery, seeing it as a threat to the British colonial system, and thus to the economic well-being of the country. He was in this, as in a number of other ways, a man of his times and of his class. However there is nothing in any of his letters to suggest that he condoned the cruelty involved with slavery – and there is certainly nothing to suggest that he supported the slave trade'.

Clearly, Dr White believed that the full text of the original letter was reproduced by Laughton in *The Naval Miscellany.* As seen in the table on p 96above, even that version of the letter, although closer to the original than most copies, was corrupted. However, Dr White's conclusions that Nelson was a man of his times and class and that there is nothing in his letters to suggest he condoned the cruelty involved in the slavery or indeed supported the slave trade, are borne out by this present study. A careful analysis of the letter to Simon Taylor, in which Nelson asks an old acquaintance for support, shows that Nelson had good military and humane reasons for his objection at that moment in time.

It should be remembered that Nelson authored a substantial number of letters, of which it is estimated that over 8,000 have been published or are known about. It would be impossible to conclude definitively that Nelson was pro-slavery from his letters as it was a subject he rarely touched upon. The evidence is fragmentary at best and highly debatable. He was clearly conservative and certainly supported the colonial system, but the evidence suggests that he would have supported that system had it been underpinned by paid rather than slave labour. With the near 'deification' of Nelson after his death it is often overlooked that Nelson was simply a serving officer, albeit a very good one. He was never senior enough to sit on the Admiralty Board and although he could have, perhaps, influenced national policy from his seat in the Lords, that opportunity never arose. His disparaging comments about Wilberforce, when seen in the context of a threat to the system in a time of heightened tension in the war with France, are entirely understandable. They should also be interpreted in the light of contemporary opinion. Wilberforce was, though revered by some today, a frequently divisive and mocked figure regardless of his abolition campaign.

Nelson's victory at Trafalgar gave the Royal Navy control of the seas. After the abolition of slavery in 1807 the Royal Navy vigorously applied the new law. Nelson, had he lived, would have seen it as his duty to apply the law with his usual force.

The Nelson-Taylor letter penned aboard HMS *Victory* in June 1805, written privately to an acquaintance[38] has been used in recent times to denigrate Nelson's reputation, leading to accusations of Nelson being a racist and pro-slavery, and assaults on representations of the Admiral, for example the defacing of his statue in Norwich.[39] However, the original letter was embellished, doctored and widely circulated by the anti-abolitionists in a last-ditch attempt to use Nelson's name and fame to influence the outcome of the Act for the Abolition of the Slave Trade. Forged copies of the letter show a number of changes and additions when compared to the original and one bears a forged seal and 'Nelson & Bronte' signature. The letter was amended for publication in Cobbett's *Political Register* in February 1807. Critics who have accused Nelson of being racist and pro-slavery have relied on these manufactured copies of the original letter which, 200 years later, continue to sway public opinion. There is no doubt that the anti-abolitionists sought to exploit Nelson's heroic and patriotic reputation to influence the abolition debate. To this end they took a private letter written to an acquaintance and altered the content of that letter in an attempt to make it seem that Nelson was unequivocally pro-slavery and would have been opposed to the Bill. Forged versions of Nelson's letter were circulated to influential members of Parliament and the Government.

Whilst the letter shows Nelson's support for the colonial system, which critics have simplistically equated as support for the slave trade which underpinned it, careful analysis shows that Nelson's inferred support for that system was bred from a long established and over-riding sense of duty rather than any fundamental personal belief. Further, his actions demonstrated a humane and pragmatic approach when directly faced with the issue of slavery. The letter confirms Nelson's concern for the stability of the system, which he saw as being undermined by Wilberforce, particularly at a time of heightened threat in the war with France. The use of the letter and Nelson's posthumous reputation by the anti-abolitionists was intended to deceive politicians of the day and, more recently, has resulted in the unjustified defamation of Nelson's character. Indeed, many today have fallen into the trap so carefully laid by the pro-slavery lobby in 1807.

PART THREE: THE FINAL BATTLE

'Words have consequences' Sir Keir Starmer, February 2022

11

FALSE HISTORY?

In Parts One and Two above the contentions that Nelson was a racist and white supremacist have been assessed, with little or no evidence being found to support those claims. Nelson did write to Simon Taylor of Jamaica seemingly vowing to oppose the abolition of the slave trade but a careful consideration and analysis of the wording of that letter shows that any support for the planters' cause was heavily conditional. There is much more to that letter than initially appears. The views expressed clearly demonstrate the concern of someone fearing the military and social consequences that would flow from abolition at that time, and these have to be set against his support for ideas to replace slave labour with paid labour. Even then the content of the letter to Simon Taylor did not satisfy the anti-abolitionists. Perhaps mindful of its equivocal nature they set about manufacturing a version of the letter and circulating this forgery in an attempt to influence public and political opinion at a critical juncture in the debates about abolition of the slave trade.

Historians in recent times have entangled Nelson in current debates about the role in the slave trade of some historic figures. Some have inadvertently drawn on the forged copies of Nelson's letter apparently without considering the reasons for differences between printed versions or Nelson's intentions in wording it as he did. This in turn has led to a number of claims which have impacted on Nelson's reputation. A sample of these claims is examined below.

Historic England

In 2018 Historic England, the public body 'that helps people care for, enjoy and celebrate England's spectacular historic environment' launched a debate about commemorations of famous historic figures entitled 'Revere or Remove'. Historic England sought to promote this debate by showing images, on Twitter, of a wrecking ball toppling the statue of Nelson from the top of Nelson's Column.

Not surprisingly a significant public outcry followed and the images were quickly removed, with a spokesman for Historic England maintaining that the organisation did not support demolishing Nelson's Column and that 'Nelson's Column was chosen (to stimulate debate) because it is so iconic and well recognised'[1]

Whilst there is justification for debate about and investigation of historic figures and their role in episodes of our history, including colonialism, slavery and the slave trade, the use of such imagery is both pejorative and unhelpful. The implication of the images is that Nelson was guilty (of something) and that, in the public mind, his statue deserves to be removed. Despite the claimed intentions of Historic England the damage was done.

It should be remembered that the memorials to Nelson, for example in the form of street names, schools and statues, commemorate his role in the defence of his country and his success in significant battles, during one of which he gave his life. In that respect, the columns and statues can be seen in the tradition of the victory columns of the ancient Roman Empire. The tens of thousands of people who lined the streets to witness Nelson's funeral 'in a spontaneous outpouring of public emotion which would not be matched until Princess Diana … died' were evidence of the importance of Nelson and his battles at the time of his death.[2] Unlike other statues, such as those of Cecil Rhodes or Edward Colston, Nelson's statues do not celebrate philanthropic or other events associated with the use of capital derived from the slave trade.

The Welsh Assembly (now the Welsh Parliament or Senedd)

In November 2020 the Welsh Assembly published an audit of commemoration in Wales, entitled *'The Slave Trade and the British Empire.*[3] The primary purpose of the audit was: 'to collect and review the evidence for aspects of our historic environment associated with black history, and in particular of the role of the British Empire and the slave trade as it applies to Wales'.

In the audit Lord Nelson is attributed to a group of 'people who opposed abolition of the slave trade' (Audit page 7). In the discussion section of the report it is stated: 'While Nelson may have condoned the slave trade privately ….. it is not clear whether ..(he)… had any responsibility for perpetuation of the slave trade' (Audit p 12).

In Annex 1 of the report, entitled 'Persons of Interest', under the 'Discussion' column, it is alleged that Nelson is 'known from private correspondence to have opposed the abolition of the slave trade though he doesn't appear to have done so publicly'. The evidence for this statement is given under the 'Sources' column and the reader is directed to the historyextra.com website. That website reproduces the article entitled 'Lord Nelson and Slavery: Nelson's Dark Side' by Christer Petley, which in turn relies on a doctored and embellished version of the original letter that Nelson penned to Simon Taylor, as demonstrated in Part Two of this study.

A further concern is the other source of information referred to in the Audit, the excellent UCL website 'Legacies of British Slave Ownership'. This records those who benefitted from compensation after the abolition of slavery in 1834. Following the link in the report to the website one is directed to a page where a certain Horatio Nelson is recorded as being the beneficiary of an award for a claim for a slave. The uncontested claim was for a sum of £19 10s 10d. However, on closer examination it can be seen that the award was made in March 1836, some 31 years after Nelson's death! The award clearly does not and could not relate to Admiral Lord Nelson but to a slave owner of the same name. It was very common for children of the period to be named after Lord Nelson in honour of his heroic deeds and reputation. Indeed a search of the data base reveals a further 21 claimants with the name Horatio, of which 8 also have the name Nelson linked with it but not as a surname (e.g. Horatio Belinfante of Jamaica; Horatio Nelson Huggins of Trinidad). 23 persons also had the surname Nelson although, as noted above, only one had the first name Horatio.

The Welsh Assembly's conclusions reflect poor historical research based on elementary mistakes and it is disappointing to find them receiving expression, unchecked, in a public consultation, especially in relation to such a sensitive issue.

Goldsmiths, University of London

Towards the end of 2021 Goldsmiths College, part of the University of London, consulted on a proposal to remove four statues from the former Deptford Town Hall, which property had been acquired by the college. One of those statues was of Admiral Lord Nelson.

The reason given by Goldsmiths for including Nelson in this consultation is summarised in the following statement:

'Lord Horatio Nelson (1758-1805) was a naval flag officer whose leadership is credited with a number of decisive British victories, particularly during the Napoleonic Wars (1803-1815). Nelson spent a large part of his career in the Caribbean and developed an affinity with the slave owners there, with evidence suggesting he used his influence to argue against the abolitionist movement in Britain.'

The argument that Nelson developed an affinity with slave owners in the Caribbean is examined in Part One of this study as is the suggestion that he used his influence to argue against the abolitionist movement in Britain. Nelson clearly did not spend a large part of his career in the Caribbean and there is thin evidence that he had a longstanding and empathetic relationship with any of the slave owners. It is regrettable that these contentions, repeated in the Goldsmiths' summary above, have been accepted at face value when no evidence has been brought forward to substantiate them, and even more regrettable that they are used as the basis for influencing public opinion and decision making.

On 12th June 2022 Goldsmiths published the findings and conclusions of the consultation. That found that 58% of the respondents to a postal consultation, involving the local community, were opposed to the removal of the statues whilst 85% of respondents to an online consultation 'strongly disagreed' or 'disagreed' with the statues' removal, Goldsmiths have therefore decided not to seek approval for the removal of the statues (approval would be required as the statues form part of a building listed as being of historical or architectural interest). Instead the college now proposes to install free standing interpretation panels on the window ledges below the statues, develop a programme of community engagement and a grant for local artists of colour to explore issues raised by the statues.

Uncomfortable Art

In June 2020 *The Telegraph* published an article (subsequently reported in *The Week* of 20th June) entitled '*All aboard Britain's "uncomfortable art" Tour'* by journalist Guy Kelly. He was reporting on historian Alice Procter's visits to 'problematic' monuments. The article states: 'In Trafalgar Square, Nelson's atop his column. It's on the topple list. Well Nelson was really, really racist. He was very pro-slavery, and wrote a letter stating that he'd essentially fight until his dying breath to stop William Wilberforce and his brethren, so we've got him in his own words'.

The quote is attributed to Procter. The statement is strong and emphatic and clearly relies on the Nelson-Taylor letter whilst misquoting it. As previously demonstrated it is not possible to draw such strident conclusions from the original letter, which must be understood both in context and with a broader assessment of Nelson's views of the colonies and how they could be serviced by free paid labour.

In her book *"The Whole Picture"* Procter considers, amongst other things, the role of monuments and who is represented by statues and who is not.[4] She discusses the role and effect of Shonibare's *Ship* which, for some time, was located on the fourth plinth in Trafalgar Square. Procter notes that the *Ship* 'challenged' the space but this comment is accompanied by the almost throwaway statement, in parentheses, that 'there was no overt critique of Nelson or his support for enslavement' in the Square.[5] If such a critique were justified it would need to be grounded in fact – facts which are sadly lacking in the book.

Later in the same chapter Procter maintains that '… British politicians including Nelson had been advocating against the abolition of slavery on the basis that it would damage their wealth'. The source for this claim is the Simon-Taylor letter reproduced in Nicolas.[6]The Nicolas letter is in any case a heavily amended version of Nelson's original (see Table above) but Procter's claim is flawed in several major respects in connection with Nelson. First, Nelson was not a politician; he was a career naval officer. His ventures into the political arena were limited, as evidenced in Part One of this study, to six speeches in the House of Lords, none of which related to the slave trade or slavery. Secondly, from the contents of the Nicolas version of the letter (or any other version for that matter) it is impossible to conclude, or even infer, that Nelson opposed abolition to maintain his wealth. (There can be no doubt that certain politicians did oppose abolition on the grounds of protecting their wealth but Nelson did not). It's a matter of simple fact that Nelson did not derive any of his wealth, such as it was, from the slave trade or slavery.

Whilst recognising that *"The Whole Picture"* was not intended as a study of Nelson, unfortunately, when such comments enter the public domain without substantiation, they can rapidly become the mantra of 'conventional wisdom', whether proven or not.

The 'mantra' as conventional wisdom

A few examples help demonstrate how this 'mantra' becomes the accepted wisdom, albeit that it is based on unsubstantiated claims and not backed up by evidence or proper analysis.

A number of schools and other educational establishments are named after celebrated historical figures who are now accused of having had links with the slave trade, and these establishments are considering re-naming as a result. Similar proposals have come forward from local authorities reviewing place and street names, a number of which are listed in '*Protecting Local Heritage*' by the Policy Exchange.[7] Nelson is included in several such proposals. Whilst local authorities may be entitled to embark on such changes, to provide more 'relevant' role models for the modern age, in doing so they should take care to ensure that, in setting out the case for change, they have regard to correct evidence, not unsubstantiated opinions and lazy history.

In June 2020 a Norfolk County Councillor sought the renaming of the Nelson Ward in Norwich in the wake of nationwide calls for the taking down of statues celebrating colonialism and the slave trade. The Councillor, who represented Nelson Ward, said it was named after Horatio Nelson 'who opposed the abolition of slavery'. Again this statement could only have been based on (reports of) the forged Simon Taylor letter. Ironically, the anti-abolitionists' forged version of Nelson's opinions has forced a re-evaluation of the very reputation they sought to exploit and still deceives people today. It should be noted that in the immediate aftermath of Nelson's death, when the forged versions of Nelson's letter came to the fore, the debates in Parliament were about the abolition of the slave trade and not the abolition of slavery. So to equate Nelson's (wrongly) purported views on the abolition of the slave trade with the abolition of slavery itself is to misunderstand the context of events in that period.

At the same time as the outcry over the re-naming of Nelson Ward, the Norfolk Naval Pillar (locally known as Nelson's Column) in Great Yarmouth, entered the debate. The Column, erected in 1819, some 24 years before Nelson's Column in Trafalgar Square, celebrates Nelson's naval victories. Local opinion suggested that the residents of Norfolk wouldn't allow Nelson's statues to be toppled and that there was little evidence for Nelson and representations of him to be embroiled in the nationwide statue debate.

A further example from Nelson's home county demonstrates how unsubstantiated assertions find their way into the public domain without challenge. In 2022, the Castle Museum in Norwich had a small Nelson exhibition in the museum's decorative arts gallery. Supporting text to an element of the display, entitled 'Nelson and British Naval Supremacy', included the following paragraph: 'In recent years, Nelson's well-known support for the slave trade in his lifetime has caused controversy. This aspect of his character, morally repugnant to us today, should neither be emphasised nor concealed. It reminds us that figures from the past, as much as from the present, should not be seen simplistically as pure heroes or villains.'

Whilst the statement sought to balance our understanding of historical figures, it clearly started from an assumption that Nelson supported the slave trade which, as has been seen, is not proven. There is no evidence of any public pronouncement by Nelson on this matter, either verbally or in writing. So it is impossible to claim that Nelson's purported support for the slave trade was well-known in his lifetime. The very few references he made to the slave trade were in private letters and were certainly not intended to influence public debate on the matter. It is only very recently that such charges have been made against Nelson, based largely on the forged Simon Taylor letter, released after Nelson's death when he was unable to make clear his position on this matter. It was Nelson's standing in the British pantheon, rather than his fundamental beliefs, that the West Indian planters were seeking to exploit, and judgements, based on their forgeries, still continue to influence historians today. Notwithstanding, as in the case of the Castle Museum, the statement was there for all to see and, no doubt, went largely unchallenged by the public at large.

More recently, Glasgow City Council launched their audit of historic connections and legacies related to slavery and Atlantic commerce.[8]This seemingly, thoroughly prepared audit nonetheless relies on statements made in Christer Petley's *'Dark Side'* article and his chapter in *'The Royal Navy and the British Atlantic World'* (referred to earlier in this study) when commenting upon Nelson. These, as has been seen, rely on corrupted versions of Nelson's original letter. This audit also displays a further characteristic of the mantra. That is, it is embellished by purported historical facts. For example, the audit states that Nelson **remained** in favour of plantation slavery. As has been seen there is no evidence that he ever supported the slave trade or favoured slavery – indeed he is known to have supported proposals for the replacement of slave labour, in the West Indies, with paid labour. Secondly the audit goes on to state: 'Nelson was, of course, a naval commander in charge of the British Navy, which included patrolling the West Indies and defending British possessions and by extension, facilitating the continuation of chattel slavery'.

As a matter of recorded fact, Nelson was never a commander in charge of the British Navy. His early tours of duty to the West Indies ended in 1787 when Nelson was but a junior captain. His final 'visit' to the West Indies was in pursuit of the French fleet, trying to bring them to battle in June 1805, when he was an Admiral of the Mediterranean fleet, but this did not include patrolling the West Indies, nor indeed setting foot on the islands (see Figure 3). Notwithstanding, the addition of such statements appears to give the 'mantra' an air of credibility. (Following contact by The Nelson Society, the author of the report has undertaken to review the section of the report relating to Nelson, having regard to the discovery of the forged letter, and to correct any historical inaccuracies).

Notwithstanding, the mantra has momentum. As recently as June 2023 *The Telegraph* drew attention to St Paul's Cathedral's website 'State Funerals: Nelson, Wellington and Churchill'. The website said of Nelson 'Over time, aspects of his character and behaviour have been assessed more critically, particularly his personal commitment to the system of slavery'. The strong inference is that Nelson supported the slavery although no evidence for this contention is offered. Following comment in *The Telegraph* the statement was amended to read 'Over time, aspects of his character and behaviour have been assessed more critically, particularly his views in relation to the slave trade'. The problem, of course, is that when respected bodies such as St Paul's repeat the mantra it is unlikely to be questioned and the unproven myth perpetuated.

National Museum of the Royal Navy (Portsmouth)

In June 2020 the Executive Director of the Museum of the Royal Navy, Matthew Sheldon, reflected on the debate surrounding historical figures and their representations, including Nelson and his views on slavery.[9] Drawing on a forged version of the Nelson-Taylor letter he concluded that, whilst Nelson's direct links to slavery were slight, his personal commitment to the system of slavery was strong. Sheldon sets out the circumstantial evidence for Nelson's views being shaped by his relationship with planters in the Caribbean and by a view current in the navy at the time that the West India merchant navy provided a training ground for the Navy, which could be called upon in times of war. (It should be noted that Nelson himself never articulated this view, although it was one expressed by other naval officers called to give evidence to the Parliamentary Inquiry into the slave trade in 1790).

Sheldon poses the question, amongst others, as to whether the museum should focus on Nelson at all when considering the connection of the Royal Navy to the slave trade. He concludes that it would be bad naval history not to include an intensive study of Nelson in its exhibitions, which in any event is warranted by Nelson's significant achievements and impact of their legacy. A forensic examination of Nelson's views on the slave trade and slavery would represent a significant component of this intensive study.

National Maritime Museum (Greenwich)

In October 2020 *The Sunday Telegraph* ran an article entitled '*Legacy review could knock Nelson off his pedestal'*. The article claimed that the National Maritime Museum would be reviewing Nelson's 'heroic status' as part of efforts to challenge Britain's 'barbaric history of race and colonialism'.[10] The *Sunday Telegraph* article was picked up by other newspapers and the Director of the National Maritime Museum appeared on BBC Radio 4's 'Today' news programme to rebut the allegations. In short the Director confirmed that Nelson's views on slavery are not certain and the content of the Nelson-Taylor letter did not give cause for any change to the Museum's presentation of Nelson's life and achievements. The Director also highlighted the danger of 'condemning' people out of the frame of reference of their times.

Understandably the presentation of Nelson and interpretation of him will change over time in response to future needs and new discoveries but the interest excited by the above episodes shows the enduring appeal and importance of Nelson in the public eye.

In the building neighbouring the National Maritime Museum at Greenwich is the Nelson Room, where Nelson's body was to rest prior to laying in state in the Painted Hall for three days before his funeral. The Nelson Room houses a small exhibition. One of the panels tackles the issue of Nelson and the slave trade thus:

'... More recently, Nelson has attracted controversy in relation to Britain's trade in enslaved people, which was abolished in 1807. In a private letter to a Jamaica-based plantation owner, Nelson criticised the 'damnable cruel doctrine' of the abolitionist William Wilberforce and expressed support for 'our present colonial system'. After Nelson's death a modified version of this letter was used in the campaign against the abolition of the slave trade'.

This seems an accurate summary of the situation as determined by this study.

Symbolism

There can be little doubt that Nelson IS associated with the age of empire and colonialism and his image, particularly as represented on Nelson's Column, has been used to draw attention to debates about race and slavery, as in the case of *The Guardian* article in 2017 and Historic England's debate.

The book '*Natives: Race and Class in the Ruins of Empire'* by Akala, was a Sunday Times bestseller, and Foyles non-fiction book of the year in 2018.[11] The cover of the hardback version is black with a blue silhouette of Nelson's Column superimposed upon it. The title of the book, in white lettering, runs top to bottom through the Column. An image of the Column, in white, is also on the spine of the book. The paperback version of the book has an image of the statue of Nelson atop the Column in Trafalgar Square, the image of the Column coloured red.

'Natives' is an intelligent examination of race and class and offers alternative views on certain aspects of British history. However, notwithstanding the prominence of Nelson on the cover, the only reference to him in the book notes that Britain has preserved HMS *Victory* as a tribute to Nelson, whilst not a single slave ship survives.[12]

At a trite level it can be noted that Nelson is a significant part of the British psyche and his image is so well known that it helps to publicise and sell books. However, the use of the image in connection with any title using the words 'race', 'slavery' or 'slave trade' infers a pejorative link between Nelson and those issues.

Nelson is inextricably linked with the age of colonialism, which in turn was supported by the slave trade and slavery. It was the age into which Nelson was born and in which he succeeded in his professional ambitions and the use of Nelson's image reinforces this connection with the colonial age in the subconscious mind.

12

CONCLUSIONS TO PART THREE

In current times Nelson's alleged support for the slave trade hangs heavily over his reputation. The question remains as to how so many respected historians and public bodies have come to believe that Nelson was pro-slavery and it is tempting to take the comfortable stance that, if so many believe it and perpetuate it, they must be right. However, the answer is clear: they have all relied on the contents of versions of the forged Nelson-Taylor letter. However, none of them appears to have been able to access the true copy of the original letter - the pressed letter – but, rather, have relied on the forged versions and subsequent interpretations or impressions of that letter. Some have taken these interpretations without challenge and repeated the 'mantra', and this is questionable history.

Had historians accessed the original (pressed copy) letter they may well have examined the differences in wording between it and later forged and published copies of the letter and considered why those changes were made and their associated meaning. Knowing that such changes had been made they would have been obliged, on the grounds of professional integrity, to query the underlying rationale behind the letter and to have considered other aspects of its context rather than just the slave trade, significant though it was, such as the wars with France. This, indeed, is the challenge to those historians and Nelson experts.

The evidence against Nelson being racist or a white supremacist is extremely thin, indeed seemingly non-existent. His approach to peoples of all ethnicities was one based on humanity and was generally compassionate. The allegation that his opposition to the abolition of slavery was absolute, and that he was therefore pro-slavery, is equally thin, being based as it is on a few lines in a private letter, where Nelson was (for specific reasons) really saying what the recipient wanted to hear. But even then that purported objection to abolition of the slave trade was heavily qualified. In the absence of any other corroborating evidence, either in deed or writing, it is difficult to conclude, as many have done, that Nelson was pro-slavery. Unfortunately the allegations have been taken as fact, pervaded the public consciousness and have been used in arguments in decision making. It should now be for his accusers to bring forward their evidence.

AFTERWORD

In recent times Britain's colonial past and its slave trade history has been the subject of extensive examination and critical debate. It has given rise to considerable study, literature and direct actions. Understandably and unavoidably, perhaps, much of the debate has been of a partisan nature and even attempts at impartiality are affected by unconscious bias. Objectivity is hard to achieve within the background clamour from all parties to the discussion and it would be foolish to try to claim immunity from bias.

Further questions arose as I undertook this study. Should historians, or writers of history, engage in moral judgements on the past? In the present case that seemed hard to avoid as morality was an integral part of the debates on the subject itself, i.e. race and slavery. The danger, of course, is that historians address the evidence with a pre-conceived 'morality' which derives from the society (our society) and times within which they exist. That certainly seems to be the case within some of the examples set out in Part Three of this work.

I embarked on this exercise hoping to prove conclusively that Nelson, one of my longstanding heroes (my bias), was neither racist nor a white supremacist. To that end I felt it important to try to find every comment he may have made on the subject of race, slavery and the slave trade, orally and in writing, and to try to understand their meaning. It was also necessary to examine his actions to see if they give an indication as to his feelings on such matters. To assist in this I have, therefore, sought to set Nelson's actions and comments 'in context'. I have found little to support the criticisms of Nelson as a racist or white supremacist. Similarly I find little to suggest that Nelson was a strong supporter of the slave trade or slavery. For the reasons I have explained, that whilst Nelson may have seemed intent on opposing the abolition of the slave trade, as he expressed in private letters of 1802 and 1805, (although he never did publicly or privately oppose abolition), he was also supportive of ideas to replace slavery in the colonies with paid labour, which seems consistent with his humanitarian, world views. All this suggests that he would have supported a measured approach to the abolition of the slave trade.

If Nelson had never written the now infamous letter to Simon Taylor, on-board Victory in June 1805, it is highly unlikely that his standing or reputation would ever have been questioned. However, he did and, in light of his significant achievements, his views and actions deserve careful and thorough consideration and analysis. Such consideration and analysis should take account of verified source material which, it seems to me, is the obligation placed on all commentators. As I stated in the Foreword, I have no doubt that this study is 'live' research and that other information will come to light which may cast a different hue on my conclusions, but in the meantime I trust this study helps illuminate the debate.

The discovery of the forged letters was a significant moment, and confirms that the West Indian planters would stop at nothing to make their case in parliament, including embroiling Nelson, posthumously, in their strategies. The possible collusion of Prince William Henry, in their efforts, comes as no surprise in light of his strident and public views on slavery and the slave trade. I am sure there is much more to uncover here. There is one sense, of course, in which Nelson could be said to 'support' the slave trade. He was a serving officer in the Royal Navy, which was an instrument of state. During Nelson's lifetime the state supported the slave trade and thus, by extension Nelson, as a naval officer, supported that trade. However, that does not mean he, personally, was in favour of that trade. The evidence suggests that, had he addressed the issue, he would have supported a carefully controlled abolition. That is, one which would not undermine the nation's efforts in its war with France, that longstanding and constant enemy, defeat of whom was his over-riding concern. It must be remembered that, despite the accusations levelled against him, Nelson never made any public pronouncements about slavery or the slave trade, and his letter to Simon Taylor was never in the public domain during his lifetime. It was a private letter that was never intended to influence public opinion.

The larger context in which Nelson operated, one of empire and colonial expansion and protectionism, is increasingly uncomfortable to early 21st century society, particularly as that context was underpinned, in part, by the Atlantic Slave Trade. It seems that, in the absence of specific or overwhelming evidence, Nelson has been used as a high profile symbol of blame for that uncomfortable context and that, in essence, it seems to me, is the true extent of the complaints against him.

Postscript:

It may seem to the Nelson enthusiast that the regular attacks on Nelson's reputation are now endless. However, at a time when statues (of him) are threatened with removal it is interesting to note that new statues to Nelson are still being erected, such as at his birthplace in Burnham Thorpe (2021) and in Chichester (2021). Perhaps it is as Daniel Hannan said (see Foreword) – the issue of Nelson and slavery is incidental to Nelson's story.

APPENDIX 1

THE PRESSED COPY OF THE ORIGINAL LETTER

(Copyright M. Downer)

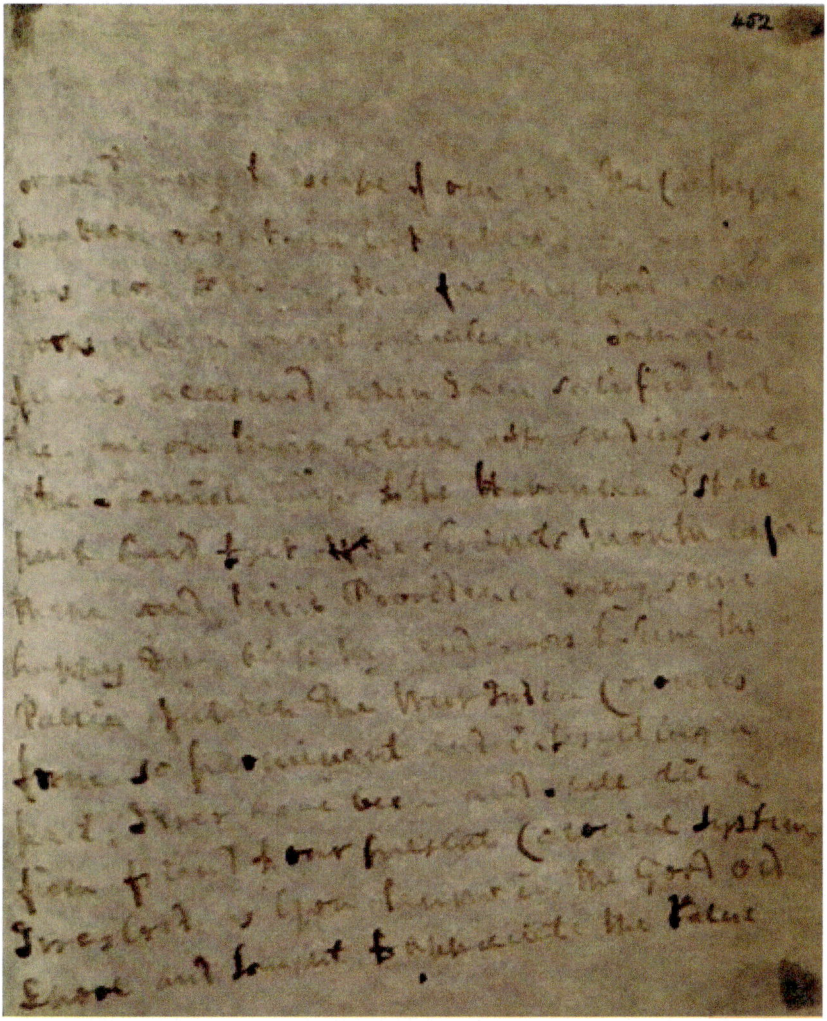

[illegible] and neither
in the first [illegible] shall be in
[illegible] I have
[illegible]
to launch my voice against the
the [illegible] (and doctrine [illegible] for
and [illegible] hypocritical allies and [illegible]
that has birth in Heaven [illegible]
exalted as him, who would [illegible]
over the Murder shall our friends
and fellow subjects in the Colonies,
I did not intend to have gone so far
however [illegible] fixed in my heart
but the sentiments [illegible]
[illegible] words [illegible]
[illegible] have done
[illegible] as [illegible]
[illegible] England for [illegible]
the [illegible]

104.

[illegible] could [illegible] time and [illegible]
has deserved be very great [illegible] from
you, [illegible] nearly [illegible] years [illegible]
time [illegible] to see my [illegible] daughter
your faithful and obliged friend [illegible]

Nelson & Bronte

The Revd Dr Scott Rector of [illegible]
is a most staunch friend [illegible]
[illegible] friend he has lost [illegible]
by [illegible]
remembrances and good wishes to you
He is a worthy good man and a very old
friend of mine. Many of my old Jamaica
friends are near you they [illegible] kindly
remembered to them

APPENDIX 2

THE DOCTORED COPY OF THE ORIGINAL LETTER SHOWING SEAL AND FORGED SIGNATURE.

(Copyright M. Downer).

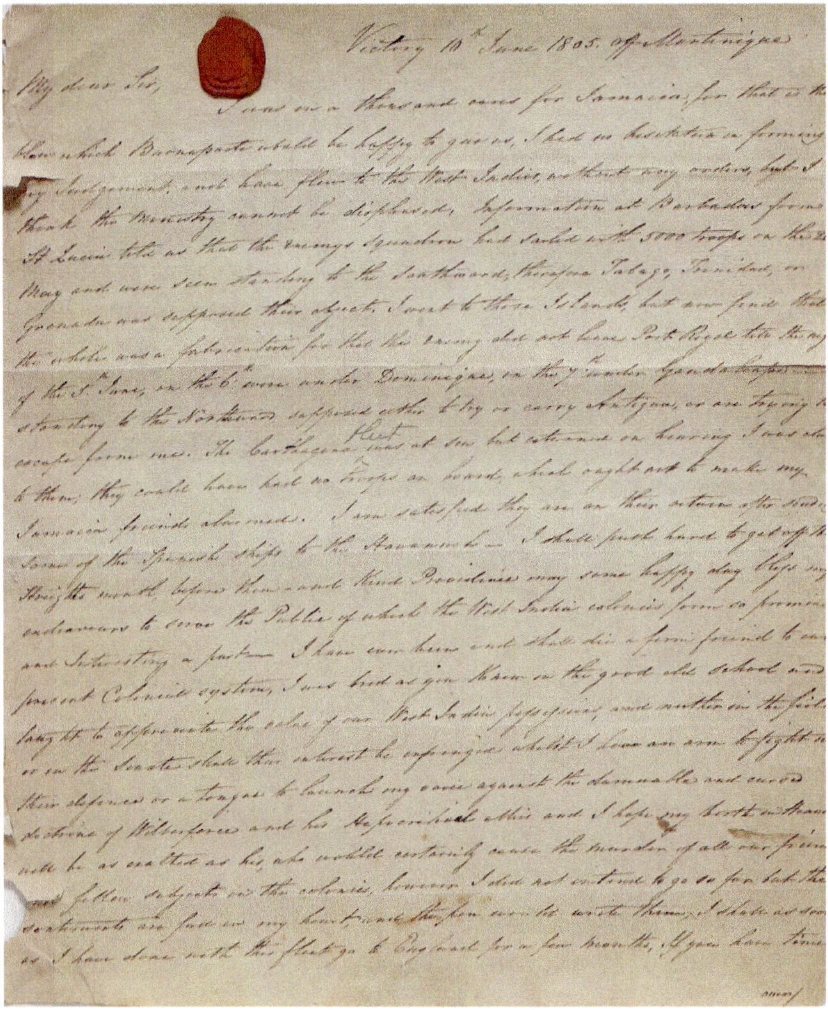

Victory 10th June 1805. off Martinique

My dear Sir,

I was in a thousand cares for Jamaica, for that is the blow which Buonaparte would be happy to give us, I had no hesitation in forming my Judgement, and have flown to the West Indies, without any orders, but I think the Ministry cannot be displeased, Information at Barbadoes from St Lucia told us that the enemys Squadron had sailed with 5000 troops on the 28 May and were seen standing to the Southward, therefore Tobago, Trinidad, or Grenada was supposed their object, I went to those Islands, but now find that the whole was a fabrication for that the enemy did not leave Port Royal till the night of the 5th June, on the 6th were under Dominique, on the 7th under Guadaloupe standing to the Northward supposed either to try or carry Antigua, or are trying to escape from me. The Carthagena fleet was at sea but returned on hearing I was after them; they could have had no troops on board, which ought not to make my Jamaica friends alarmed. I am satisfied they are on their return after sending some of the Spanish ships to the Havannah – I shall push hard to get off the Streights mouth before them – and kind Providence may some happy day bless my endeavours to serve the Public of which the West India colonies form so prominent and Interesting a part – I have ever been and shall die a firm friend to our present Colonial system, I was bred as you know in the good old school and taught to appreciate the value of our West India possessions, and neither in the field or in the Senate shall their interest be infringed whilst I have an arm to fight in their defence or a tongue to launch my voice against the damnable and cursed doctrine of Wilberforce and his Hypocritical allies and I hope my berth in Heaven will be as exalted as his, who would certainly cause the murder of all our friends and fellow subjects in the colonies, however I did not intend to go so far but the sentiments are full in my heart and the pen would write them, I shall as soon as I have done with this fleet go to England for a few months, If you have time

any/

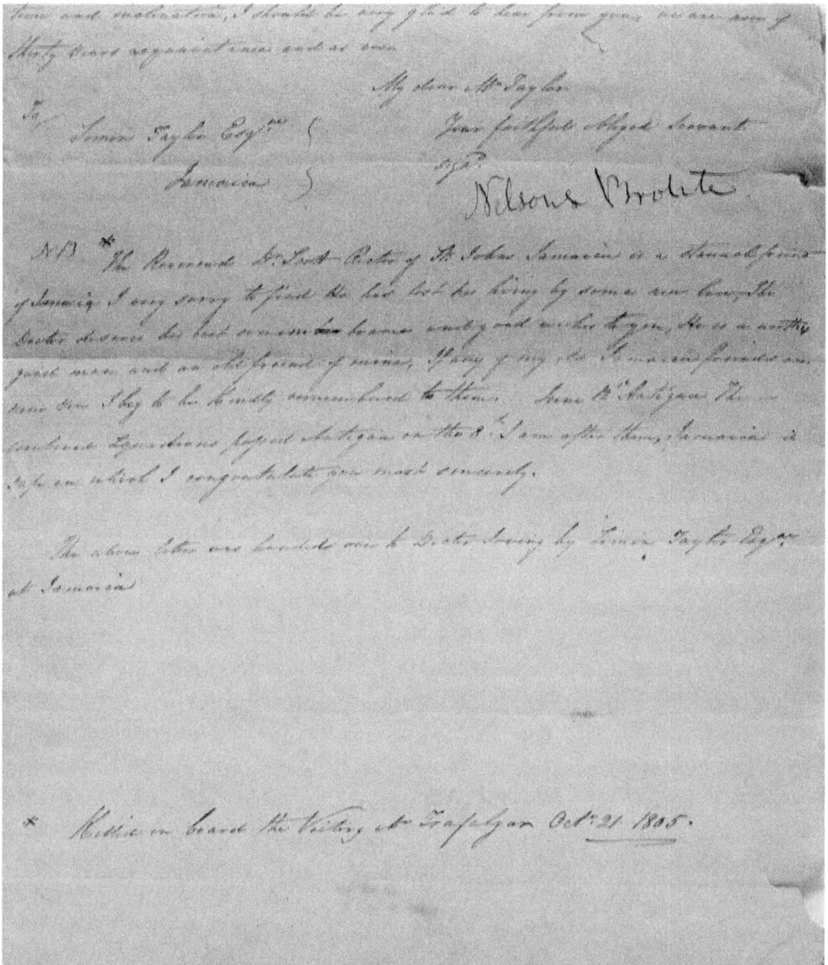
time and inclination; I should be very glad to hear from you, we are now of thirty years acquaintance and as ever

My dear Mr Taylor

Your faithful obliged servant

Signd Nelson & Bronte

To Simon Taylor Esqre Jamaica

N.B. * The Reverend Dr. Scott Rector of St. John Jamaica is a staunch friend of Jamaica, I am sorry to find he has lost his living by some new laws, the Doctor deserves his best [illegible] and my good wishes to you, he is a worthy good man and an old friend of mine, if any of my old Jamaica friends are near you I beg to be kindly remembered to them. Since the Antigua the combined Squadrons passed Antigua on the 8th I am after them, Jamaica is safe on which I congratulate you most sincerely.

The above letter was handed over to Doctor [illegible] by Simon Taylor Esqre at Jamaica

* Killed on board the Victory at Trafalgar Octr 21 1805.

APPENDIX 3

NELSON - TAYLOR FORGERY – NMRN Version

Transcript of the doctored handwritten copy of the letter from Lord Nelson to Mr Simon Taylor of Jamaica dated June 10th 1805 (Original spelling maintained)

"Victory 10th June 1805 off Martinique
My Dear Sir
I was in a thousand cares for Jamaica for that is the blow which Buonaparte would be happy to give us. I had no hesitation in forming my judgement, and have flew to the West Indies without any orders, but I think the Ministry cannot be displeased.

Information at Barbadoes from St Lucia told us, that the enemy's squadron had sailed with 5000 troops on the 20thMay and were seen standing to the Southward, therefore Tobago, Trinidad, or Granada was supposed their object. I went to those islands, but now find that the whole was a fabrication, for that the enemy did not leave Port Royal till the night of the 5thJune, on the 6th were under Dominiqua, on the 7th under Guadaloupe standing to the Northward, supposed either to try or carry Antigua, or are trying to escape from me. The Carthagena fleet was at sea, but returned on hearing I was close to them; they could have had no troops on board which ought not to make my Jamaica friends alarmed. I am satisfied they are on their return, after sending some of the Spanish ships to the Havanah. I shall push hard to get off the Straights mouth before them, and Kind Providence may some happy day bless my endeavours to serve the Public of which the West India colonies form so prominent and interesting a part. I have ever been, and shall die a firm friend to our present Colonial system. I was bred as you know in the good old school, and taught to appreciate the value of our West India possessions, and neither in the field or in the Senate shall their interest be infringed whilst I have an arm to fight in their defence or a tongue to launch my voice against the damnable and cursed doctrine of Wilberforce and his hypocritical allies, and I hope my berth in Heaven will be as exalted as his, who would certainly cause the murder of all our friends and fellow subjects in the colonies; however I did not intend to go so far but the sentiments are full in my heart, and the pen would write them. I shall as soon as I have done with this fleet go to England for a few months. If you have time and inclination, I should be very glad to hear from you we are near of thirty years acquaintance, and as ever

My dear Mr Taylor
Your faithful obliged servant
Sign
Nelson and Bronte
NB*

The Rev Dr Scott, Rector of St John's, Jamaica is a staunch friend of Jamaica. I very sorry to find he has lost his living by some new law. The Doctor desires his best remembrances and good wishes to you; he is a worthy good man, and an old friend of mine. If any of my old Jamaica friends are near you, I beg to be kindly remembered to them. June 12th Antigua. The combined squadrons passed Antigua on the 8th, I am after them. Jamaica is safe on which I congratulate you most sincerely.

The above letter was handed over to Doctor Irving by Simon Taylor Esq at Jamaica.

*Killed on board the Victory at Trafalgar Oct 21st 1805."

APPENDIX 4

COBBETT'S POLITICAL REGISTER VERSION

This version of the letter appeared in the Political Register on 21st February 1807.Image from the public domain.

Abolition Bill.

295] POLITICAL REGISTER.—*Slave Trade.* [296

I am well aware of the state of your m upon such an occasion; and I regret, that any consideration whatever should have made you consent so to enthral yourself. Your lordship once said, in proposing a reform of parliament, that, in spite of "the *calumnious* assertion, that, if you were *in power*, you would be the last to propose such a measure, you should proceed in the discharge of your duty." Was the assertion "*calumnious*," my lord? Here, my lord, it is that our malady lies. Here are the seeds of death. It is the all-subduing system of Pitt. "What," said Sir F. Burdett, in the debate just referred to (26 March, 1797). "What was the cause of the French revolution? The progress of reason and philosophy? Reason and philosophy can boast of no such influence over mankind The revolution was caused by the extravagance, profligacy, and insolence of the administration. The same causes are operating with us; and highly as I esteem the talents of the Right Hon. Gent. (Mr. Fox), *even he could do nothing substantial for the benefit of the people, were he minister to-morrow, without an entire change in our system of politics; nor, even then, unless there be a full and free representation of the people in parliament.*" Perhaps, my lord, that this, which was said in support of your motion, you will *now* call jacobinism; but, be assured, that every honest and sensible man in the country will say, that events have fully proved it to be *true*.

SLAVE TRADE.

Copy of a Letter from Lord Nelson *to Mr. Simon Taylor of Jamaica, dated, Victory off Martinico, June* 10, 1805.

Dear Sir,——I was in a thousand fears for Jamaica; for that is a blow which Buonaparté would be happy to give us. I had no hesitation in forming my judgment, and I flew to the West Indies without any orders; but, I think the ministry cannot be displeased. Information at Barbadoes from St. Lucia told us, that the enemy's squadron had sailed with 5000 troops on the 28th of May, and were seen standing to the Southward, therefore, Tobago, Trinidad, or Grenada was supposed their object. I went to these islands, but now find the whole was a fabrication, for the enemy did not leave Fort Royal till the night of the 5th of June. On the 6th they were under Dominica. On the 7th under Guadaloupe standing to the northward, supposed either to try and carry Antigua, or are trying to escape from me. The Carthagena squadron was at sea, but returned on hearing I was close to them. They could have no troops that ought to make my Jamaica friends alarmed. When I am satisfied they are on their return, after sending some of the Spanish ships to the Havannah, I shall push hard to get off the Streights before them, and kind Providence may some happy day bless my endeavours to serve the empire, of which the West India colonies form so prominent and interesting a part. I have ever been, and shall die a firm friend to our colonial system. I was bred as you know in the good old school, and taught to appreciate the value of our West India possessions, and neither in the field nor in the senate, shall their interest be infringed while I have an arm to fight in their defence or a tongue to launch my voice against the damnable and cursed doctrine of * * * * * and his hypocritical allies, and I hope my birth in heaven will be as exalted as his, who would certainly cause the murder of all our friends and fellow subjects in the colonies; however, I did not intend to go so far; but the sentiments are full in my heart, and the pen would write them.—I shall as soon as I have done with this fleet go to England for a few months, and if you have time and inclination, I shall be glad to hear from you; we are near thirty years acquainted, and I am as ever, &c.——(Signed)——Nelson and Bronte.

12th of June off Antigua. The combined squadrons passed here on the 8th, and I am after them. Jamaica is safe, on which I congratulate you most sincerely.

ORDNANCE OFFICE.

Sir,——A proposal, revolting to the feelings and judgment of a large and estimable portion of the military force of the country, having appeared in your last Register, under the signature, Philo-Register, dated 8th November last, I rely on your candour for the admission of a few remarks on it. The writer alluded to, evidently sensible of the obnoxious tendency of his intentions, assumes the disguise of an old woman, interested in the fate of the funds, and affecting anxiety for your advice to avert apprehended ruin by their failure. Instead, however, of waiting for the guidance solicited, this sagacious writer offers a remedy for all the embarrassments of our financial system, in aid of the economy recommended by you: and expecting (like an ostrich covering its eyes to escape being seen) that the borrowed petticoat of the old woman will hide the jack-boots of the horse guards, seriously suggests that great saving of expence and much general improvement would be effected, by trans-

APPENDIX 5

THE CAMPBELL FORGERY (Copyright Chris Brett)

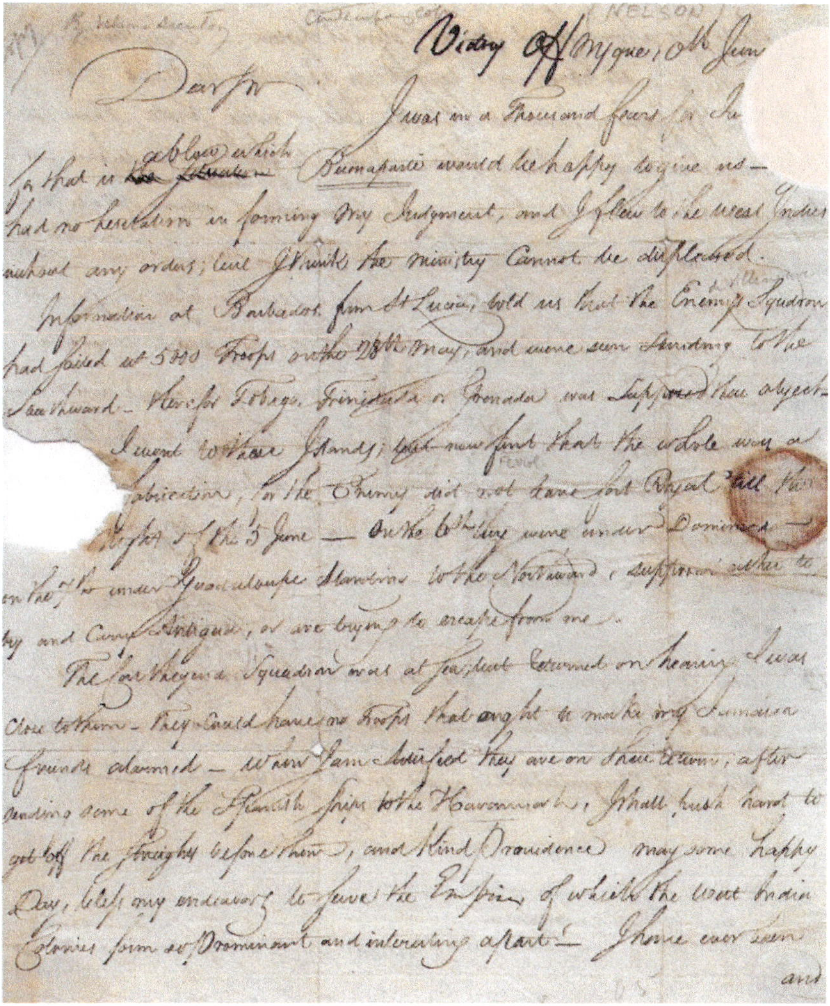
Victory off Montserrat(?), 8th June

Dear Sir

I was in a Thousand fears for the

for that is a blow which Bunaparte would be happy to give us —
had no hesitation in forming my Judgment, and I flew to the West Indies
without any orders; but I think the ministry Cannot be displeased.
Information at Barbadoes from St Lucia, told us that the Enemy's Squadron
had sailed with 5000 Troops on the 28th May, and were seen standing to the
Southward — therefore Tobago, Trinidada or Grenada was supposed their object —
I went to those Islands; but now find that the whole was a
fabrication, for the Enemy did not leave Fort Royal till the
Night of the 5 June — On the 6th they were under Dominica —
on the 7th under Guadaloupe standing to the Northward, supposed either to
try and carry Antigua, or are trying to escape from me.
The Carthagena Squadron was at Sea, but returned on hearing I was
Close to them — They could have no Troops that ought to make my Jamaica
friends alarmed — Whilst I am satisfied they are on their return, after
sending some of the Spanish ships to the Havannah, I shall push hard to
get off the Streights before them, and kind Providence may some happy
Day, bless my endeavours to serve the Empire of which the West India
Colonies form so Prominent and interesting a part — I have ever been
and

and shall Die a firm friend to our Colonial System — I was bred, as you know, in the good old school, and taught to appreciate the Value of our West India Possessions, and neither in the field or in the Senate, shall their Interest be infringed, whilst I have an arm to fight in their defence or a Tongue to launch my Voice against the Damnable Cursed Doctrine of Wilberforce and his hypocritical allies, and I hope my Birth in Heaven will be as exalted as his, who would certainly Cause the Murder of all our friends and fellow Subjects in the Colonies — however, I did not intend to go so far but the sentiments are full in my Heart, and the pen would write them.

I shall as soon as I have done with this Fleet go to England for a few months, and if you have time & inclination to [illegible] I shall be glad to hear from you — we are near 30 years acquainted & I am as ever —

Nelson & Bronte

12th June Off Antigua — The Combined Squadrons passed here on the 8th, and I am after them — Jamaica is safe on which I congratulate you most sincerely

[illegible] R.H. Earl CAMDEN

Sir John Jeffreys PRATT (1759–1840) Sec of War 1804/1805

APPENDIX 6

TRANSCRIPT OF CAMPBELL FORGERY (original spelling maintained)

"Victory Off Mque, 10th June
Dear Sir
I was in a thousand fears for Jamaica for that is a blow which Buonaparte would be happy to give us-I had no hesitation in forming my judgement, and I flew to the West Indies without any orders; but I think the ministry cannot be displeased.
Information at Barbados from St. Lucia told us that the enemy's squadron had sailed with 5,000 troops on the 28th May and were seen standing to the southward – therefore Tobago, Trinidad or Grenada was supposed their object. I went to those islands but now find that the whole was a fabrication, for the enemy did not leave Fort Royal 'till the night of the 5th June. On the 6th they were under Dominica, on the 7th under Guadaloupe standing to the northward, supposed either to try and carry Antigua or are trying to escape from me.
The Carthegena squadron was at sea but returned on hearing I was close to them they could have no troops that ought to make my Jamaican friends alarmed. When I am satisfied they are on their return after sending some of the Spanish ships to the Havannah I shall push hard to get off the straits before them, and Kind Providence may some happy day bless my endeavours to serve the Empire of which the West India Colonies form so dominant and interesting a part. I have ever been and shall die a firm friend to our colonial system. I was bred as you know in the good old school, and taught to appreciate the value of our West Indian possessions and neither in the field or in the senate shall their interest be infringed while I have an arm to fight in their defence of tongue to launch my voice against the damnable and cursed doctrine of Wilberforce and his hypocritical allies, and I hope my berth in heaven will be as exalted as his, who would certainly cause the murder of all our friends and fellow subjects in the colonies. However, I did not intend to go so far but the sentiments are full in my heart and the pen would write them.

I shall as soon as I have done with this fleet go to England for a few months and if you have time and inclination I should be very glad to hear from you. We are near 30 years acquainted and I am as ever N.&Bronte

12th June off Antigua. The combined squadrons passed here on the 8th and I am after them. Jamaica is safe on which I congratulate you most sincerely"

APPENDIX 7

THE VERSION OF THE LETTER AS IT APPEARS IN CLARKE &McARTHUR (VOL. 3 p104, 1840) (Original spelling and punctuation retained)

"My dear Sir: I was in a thousand fears for Jamaica, for that is a blow which Buonaparte would be happy to give us. I flew to the West Indies without any orders, but I think the ministry cannot be displeased... When I am satisfied that they are on their return, after sending some of the Spanish ships to the Havanna, I shall push hard to get off the Straits' mouth; *and kind Providence may some happy day bless my endeavours to serve the public weal,* of which the West India colonies form so prominent and interesting a part. I ever have been and shall die a firm friend to our present colonial system. I was bred as you know in the good old school, and taught the value of our West India possession; and neither in the field nor in the senate shall their just rights be infringed, whilst I have an arm to fight in their defence, or a tongue to launch my voice. We are nearly, my dear Mr Taylor, thirty years acquaintance; and I am, as ever, your faithful and obliged friend."

APPENDIX 8

THE VERSION OF THE LETTER AS IT APPEARS IN SIR NICHOLAS HARRIS NICOLAS (VOL. 6 pp 450-1, 1846)

"My dear Sir: I was in a thousand fears for Jamaica, for that is a blow which Buonaparte would be happy to give us. I flew to the West Indies without any orders, but I think the ministry cannot be displeased... When I am satisfied that they are on their return, after sending some of the Spanish ships to the Havanna, I shall push hard to get off the Straits' mouth; and kind Providence may some happy day bless my endeavours to serve the Public Weal, of which the West India Colonies form so prominent and interesting a part. I ever have been, and shall die, a firm friend to our present Colonial system. I was bred as you know in the good old school, and taught the value of our West India possessions; and neither in the field, nor in the senate, shall their just rights be infringed, whilst I have an arm to fight in their defence, or a tongue to launch my voice. We are nearly, my dear Mr Taylor, thirty years acquaintance; and I am, as ever, your faithful and obliged friend.
NELSON AND BRONTE"

APPENDIX 9

THE VERSION OF THE LETTER AS IT APPEARS IN LAUGHTON'S 'THE NAVAL MISCELLANY' (VOL. 1 pp438-39, 1901)

"Victory, off Martinique, 11thJune, 1805

My Dear Sir, -I was in a thousand cares for Jamaica, for that is the blow which Buonaparte would be happy to give us. I had no hesitation in forming my judgement, and I flew to the West Indies without any orders, but I think the Ministry cannot be displeased. Information at Barbadoes from St Lucia told us, that the enemy's squadron had sailed with 5000 troops on the 28th May and were seen standing to the southward; therefore Tobago, Trinidad, or Granada was supposed their object. I went to those islands, but now find that the whole was a fabrication, for that the enemy did not leave Fort Royal till the night of the 5th of June; on the 6th were under Dominica, on the 7th under Guadaloupe, standing to the northward, supposed either to try or carry Antigua, or on trying to escape from me. The Cartagena squadron was at sea, but returned on hearing I was close to them; they could have had no troops on board which ought to make my Jamaica friends alarmed. When I am satisfied they are on their return after sending some of the Spanish ships to the Havana. I shall push hard to get off the Straits' mouth before them, and kind Providence may some happy day bless my endeavours to serve the public of which the West India colonies form so prominent and interesting a part.

I have ever been and shall die a firm friend to our present colonial system. I was bred, as you know, in the good old school, and taught to appreciate the value of our West India possessions; and neither in the field or in the senate shall their interest be infringed whilst I have an arm to fight in their defence or a tongue to launch my voice against the damnable and cursed doctrine of Wilberforce and his hypocritical allies; and I hope my berth in heaven will be as exalted as his, who would certainly cause the murder of all our friends and fellow-subjects in the colonies. However I did not intend to go so far, but the sentiments are full in my heart and the pen would write them.

I shall, as soon as I have done with this fleet, go to England for a few months; and if you have time and inclination, I shall be very glad to

hear from you. We are now of thirty years acquaintance, and as ever, my dear Mr Taylor
Your faithful obliged servant
Nelson and Bronte

The Rev Dr. Scott, rector of St John's, Jamaica, is a staunch friend of mine; I am very sorry to find he has lost his living by some new law. The Doctor desires his best remembrances and good wishes to you; he is a worthy and good man, and an old friend of mine. If any of my old Jamaica friends are near you, I beg to be kindly remembered to them. June 12th Antigua. The combined squadrons passed Antigua on the 8th, I am after them. Jamaica is safe, on which I congratulate you most sincerely."

APPENDIX 10

TIMELINE

10 June 1805 - Letter to Taylor penned by Nelson aboard *HMS Victory*
21 October 1805 – Death of Nelson at Trafalgar
1806 –Taylor's 'doctored' copy of letter in circulation (?)
1806 – The 'Campbell' forgery in circulation (?)
2 Jan 1807 – First reading of the Act for the Abolition of the Slave Trade('the Act') in the House of Lords
5Feb 1807 –Second reading of the Act in the Lords, passed by 100 votes to 34
10 Feb 1807 – Third reading of the Act in the Lords; bill passed and goes to the Commons
21 Feb 1807 - Amended version of letter appears in Cobbett's *Political Register*
23 - 24 Feb – First reading of the Act in the Commons, passed by 283 votes to 16
28 Feb 1807 – Second reading of the Act in the Commons
16 Mar 1807 – Third reading of the Act in the Commons
25Mar 1807 – Act receives Royal Assent
1May 1807 – The Act for the Abolition of the Slave Trade comes into force
1809 - Reference to letter in footnote to Abolition Act debate in *Annual Register* for 1807 (p113) (actually published in 1809)
1809 - Letter referred to in Court martial of Sir Home Popham in the *Annual Register* for March 1807
1831 A version of the letter appears in the pamphlet *False sanctity*
1840 - A version of the letter appears in 2nd edition of Clarke and McArthur's *Life of Admiral Lord Nelson*
1846 Heavily redacted version of the letter appears in Nicolas *The Letters and Dispatches of Admiral Lord Viscount Nelson (Vol 6)*
1901- Copy of doctored letter published in *The Naval Miscellany* Vol 1 pp438-9
2016 – Doctored copy of the letter (referenced from *The Naval Miscellany*) referred to in Chapter 5 of '*The Royal Navy and the British Atlantic World c 1750-1820*' (Palgrave Macmillan 2016).

22 August 2017 – Afua Hirsch accuses Nelson of being a 'white supremacist' in an article in *The Guardian* newspaper entitled '*Toppling Statues? Here's why Nelson's Column should be next'*. No reference is made to the letter in the article.

24 August 2017 –Oblique reference to content of letter in article by Max Hastings in the *Daily Mail* in response to Afua Hirsch's allegations in *The Guardian*

December 2018 – The doctored version of letter referred to by Christer Petley in his article entitled '*Nelson's Dark Side'* published in the BBC's *History Magazine* Christmas edition.

18June 2020 – Doctored version of the letter referred to 'Nelson on a Pedestal' by Matthew Sheldon, Executive Director of Operations for the National Museum of the Royal Navy.

22August 2020 – Letter referred to in *The Eastern Daily Press* article '*Nelson Statue Vandalism Cost £2400 to Clean Up'*

16 September 2020 – The doctored version of the letter features in Channel 5's documentary '*Nelson: Britain's Great Naval Hero'*.

2020 onwards – the letter is alluded to or referenced in various reports/articles as discussed in Part Three of this book

APPENDIX 11

LETTER TO LORD NELSON FROM SIMON TAYLOR 15TH OCTOBER 1802

In October 1802 Simon Taylor wrote to Nelson (Ref Eg.1634 f.34) It is in this letter that Taylor set out the horrific events taking place in San Domingo.

The letter is interesting in several other respects. Taylor starts the letter by stating:

"*I am favored with your Lordship's kind letter to me of 12th July informing me your Lordship had seen Mr Pedly who informed your Lordship that I am still alive'*. He goes on to say '.. *I am much afraid and indeed know that we unhappy Colonists will want the aid and assistance of every Friend we have in the new parliament for Mr Addington's Speech on 27th May seems to prognosticate to us nothing but evil. Indeed if there is not a total new system adopted towards the Colonies to what has been followed and carried on for many years past, they will become altogether useless to Britain as they must be abandoned by the white inhabitants for it will be impossible to carry on the culture of them from the number of impediments that are in their way. Myself and our whole Country must consider ourselves under the highest Obligation to your Lordship for your intended support of us in the arduous trial that we expect will come within the next session of Parliament and consider it will decide whether in future Britain shall have West India colonies or nor or whether 80 millions of Sterling and the lives of all white people in them are to be sacrificed or not....*".

There are several points to note in respect of this letter. Nelson's letter of July 1802 was written during the Peace of Amiens (March 1802-May1803) a period during which Nelson was settled at Merton and attending the House of Lords. Mr Pedly is, therefore, quite possibly Mr John Pedley MP and Jamaican plantation owner. There is no record of Pedley having visited Merton and it is more likely that Nelson came across him in Parliament. The statement that Pedley advised Nelson that Taylor was still alive tends to confirm the proposition that Taylor and Nelson were not close and did not correspond on a regular basis, otherwise Nelson would have been aware of Taylor's 'mortality'.

In the letter Taylor clearly rehearses the arguments that the planters were seeking to use to influence debates in Parliament and uses the somewhat vitriolic language characteristic of the planters' campaign: the colonies would be '*useless to Britain';* Mr Addington's speech prognosticates '*nothing but evil': 'impossible to carry on the culture of them'* and so on.

It appears from the letter that Nelson had expressed, in his letter of July, an intention to support the colonists' case in Parliament. Mr Addington's speech of 27th May referred to the abolition of slavery in Trinidad, which in turn brought forward Lt Layman's proposals for that island, and the wider West Indies, of which Nelson knew and supported (see Part Two of this study). As evidenced in Part One Nelson did not address the subject of abolition of the slave trade in Parliament although it appears that he had the opportunity to do so when Mr Addington made his statement in the May (Nelson had been attending the House of Lords since November 1801. He almost certainly could have spoken had he felt passionately about the issue).

Regrettably the letter penned by Nelson does not appear to be in the public domain. There is no reference to it in either Nicolas or Clark and McArthur and a copy doesn't seem to appear in the volumes of pressed letters (probably because Nelson lacked secretarial support during this period of respite from war, during the Peace of Amiens). There also appears to be a gap in the pressed letters from 1796 to August 1803. It is not possible, therefore, to see if Nelson's offer of support was qualified in any way. It is possible, of course, that the letter has been destroyed. A letter of unqualified support for the planters would have been extremely useful in the debates in the run up to the votes on the abolition of the slave trade in the period 1802-1807 and would undoubtedly have been used had it existed.

APPENDIX 12

A NOTE ON NELSON'S HANDWRITING

An obvious starting point when considering whether or not the NMRN version of Nelson's letter to Simon Taylor was genuine was an examination of the handwriting. Nelson was naturally right handed. However he lost his right arm in the abortive attack on Santa Cruz in Tenerife in July 1797 and, understandably, his handwriting changed significantly as he learned to write with his left hand.

Felix Pryor (in *'Nelson the Letter Writer',* The Nelson Companion p.169, Royal Naval Museum Publications, 1995) describes Nelson's handwriting before the amputation as fairly conventional for the time 'being a fluid cursive, sloping from left to right'. After the amputation his writing becomes 'squarish' with a tendency to slope backwards and, as Pryor notes, it becomes distinctive and difficult to confuse with any hand of the period. A comparison of Nelson's handwriting in 1805, below, with that of the NMRN and Campbell letters and his letter to John Herbert in 1790 (Appendices 2, 5 and 13)) shows that these were written by different hands. The question arose as to whether the NMRN copy could have been dictated by Nelson to his Secretary, John Scott, and signed by him, as the signature looks similar to Nelson's. However, close examination of the contents of the letter shows that this was not possible.

After signing the original letter Nelson makes a plea to Simon Taylor effectively seeking the re-instatement to an ecclesiastical post for the Reverend Dr (Alexander) Scott. This plea is reproduced in the NMRN copy letter but with a further footnote that Scott was killed at Trafalgar. The footnote is in the same handwriting as the remainder of the letter. This demonstrates that this version of the letter was written **after** news of the battle reached Jamaica on 28th December 1805 but before it could be confirmed that it was Nelson's Secretary John Scott, and not his chaplain Alexander Scott, who was killed in the battle. Of course, as Nelson's Secretary was killed in the battle, it could not have been his hand that penned the letter and, if the footnote were contemporary with the remainder of the letter, the letter could

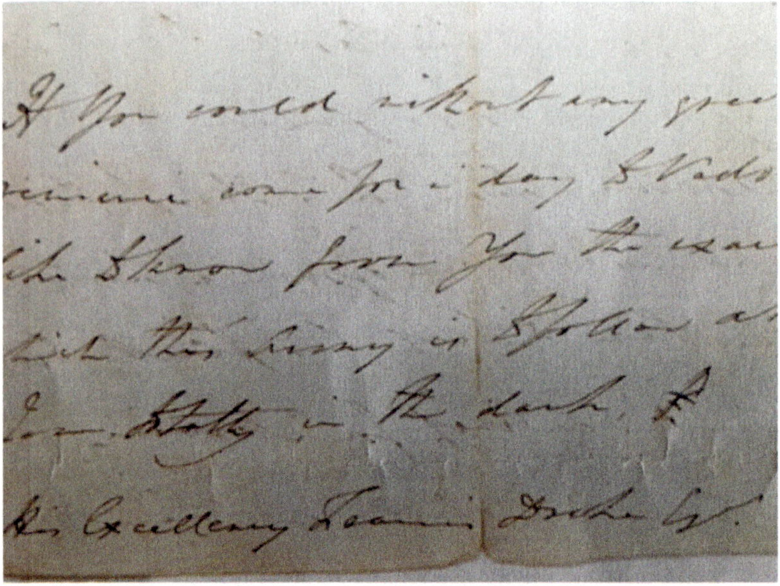

A sample of Nelson's handwriting pre-amputation

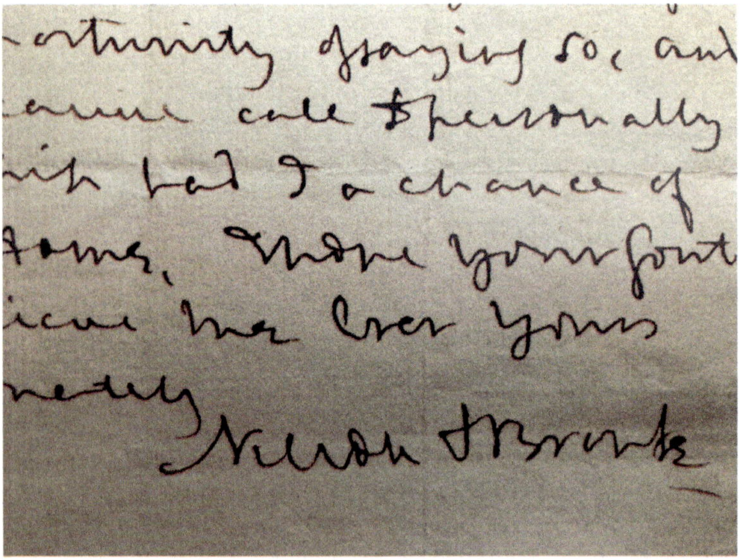

Example of Nelson's handwriting post-amputation

not have been signed by Nelson as he too had been slain at Trafalgar. Could the letter have been penned by anyone else on HMS *Victory* and the footnote have been added after the battle by them? This theory can also be dismissed. Anybody present on HMS *Victory* after the battle would have known of the death of John Scott and would not have made the fundamental mistake of asserting the death of Alexander Scott. An assessment of the handwriting clearly confirms the forging of Nelson's original letter.

In some of Nelson's letters the odd word is indecipherable. This is not surprising given that Nelson had to learn to write with the 'other' hand, and that the letters were often written on a rolling ship, in poor light and after long days of performing his naval duties.

APPENDIX 13

Nelson Letter to John Herbert, February 28th, 1790 (Copyright Martyn Downer).

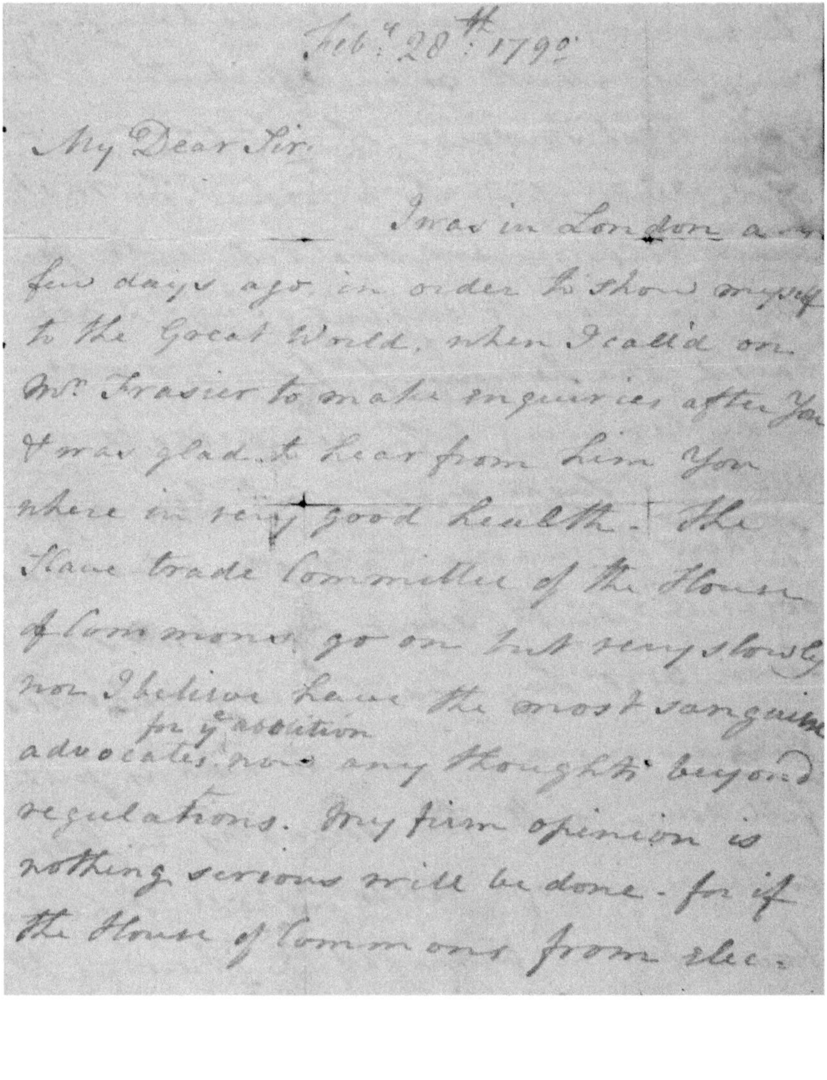

Feby. 28th: 1790.

My Dear Sir,

I was in London a
few days ago in order to show myself
to the Great World, when I call'd on
Mr. Frasier to make enquiries after You
& was glad to hear from him You
where in very good health. The
Slave trade Committee of the House
of Commons go on but very slowly
nor I believe have the most sanguine
advocates for ye abolition now any thoughts beyond
regulations. My firm opinion is
nothing serious will be done - for if
the House of Commons from elec-

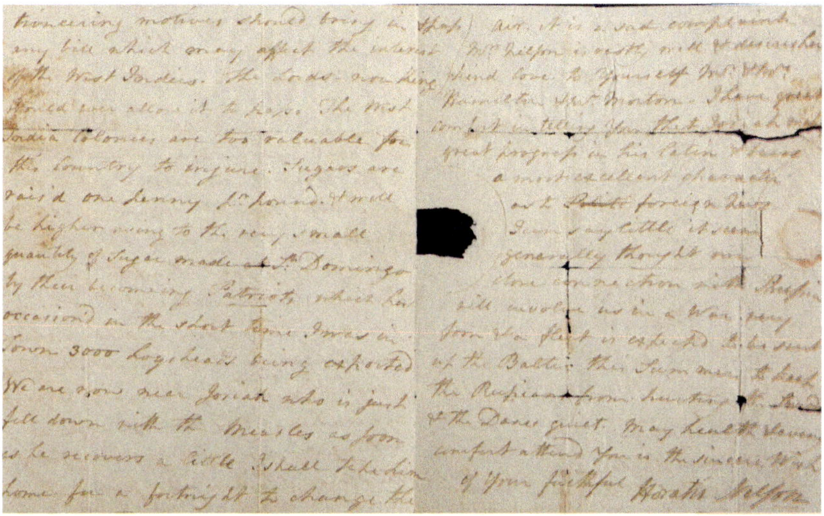

tionceering motives should bring in (that) any bill which may affect the interest of the West Indies. The Lords nor King would ever allow it to pass. The West India Colonies are too valuable for this country to injure. Sugars are rais'd one penny pr pound. & will be higher owing to the very small quantity of Sugar made at St Domingo by their becoming Patriots which has occasion'd in the short time I was in Town 3000 hogsheads being exported. We are now near Josiah who is just fell down with the Measles as soon as he recovers a little I shall take him home for a fortnight to change the

air. It is a sad complaint. Mrs Nelson is pretty well & desires her kind love to yourself Mr & Mrs Hamilton & Mr Morton. I have great comfort in telling you that Josiah makes great progress in his Latin & bears a most excellent character

as to ~~Politics~~ foreign News I know very little it seems generally thought our close connection with Russia will involve us in a War very soon the fleet is expected to be sent up the Baltic their seem meant to keep the Russians from hurting the Swedes & the Danes quiet. May health & every comfort attend you is the sincere Wish of Your faithful Horatio Nelson

I have only receiv'd one letter from You since You left England.

John R. Herbert Esqr
Nevis
Leeward Islands
West Indies.

Horatio Nelson
28th Feby 1790
not Answered

APPENDIX 14

TRANSCRIPT OF NELSON'S LETTER TO JOHN HERBERT ONNEVIS..... (Original spelling and punctuation maintained).

Feb 28 1790

My Dear Sir.

I was in London a few days ago in order to show myself to the Great World, when I call'd on M^r. Frasier to make enquiries after you& was glad to hear from him you where in very good health, The Slave trade Committee of the House of Commons go on but very slowly nor I believe have the most sanguine advocates for ye abolition nor any thoughts beyond regulations, My firm opinion is nothing serious will be done, for if the House of Commons from electioneering motives should bring in any bill which may affect the interests of the West Indies, The Lords, nor King would ever allow it to pass. The West India Colonies are too valuable for this Country to injure, Sugars are rais'd one penny per pound, &will be higher owing to the very small quantity of Sugar made at S^n: Domingo by their becoming *Patriots* which has occasion'd in the short time I was in Town 3000 hogsheads being exported We are now near Josiah who is just fell down with the measles as soon as he recovers a little I shall take him home for a fortnight to change the air, it is a sad complaint. M^rs: Nelson is mostly well & desires her kind love to yourself M^r. & M^rs:Hamilton & M^r: Morton. I have great comfort in telling you that Josiah making great progress in his latin & bears a most excellent characters to foreign news I can say little it seems generally thought our close connection with Prussia will involve us in a War very soon & a fleet is expected to be sent up the Baltic this Summer to keep the Russians from hurting the Swedes& the Danes quiet, May health & every comfort attend you is the sincere Wish of your faithful

Horatio Nelson.

I have only received one letter from you since you left England

ENDNOTES

Foreword

1. *The Guardian* 22nd August 2017.
2. Christer Petley '*Nelson and Slavery: Nelson's Dark Side' BBC History Magazine*, December 2018.
3. Sir Nicholas Harris Nicolas *The Dispatches and Letters of Vice Admiral Lord Viscount Nelson* (1844-47) , Laughton *Naval Miscellany* (1901) and Clarke and McArthur *The Life and Times of Admiral Lord Nelson* (1840)
4. Sathnam Sanghera *Empireland*, Penguin 2021, p40).
5. By 'racism' I mean the adverse mental, verbal and physical treatment of someone on the basis of the colour of their skin or ethnicity. The concept of 'white supremacy' appears based on a mis-application of Darwinist theory: the British Empire proved the superiority of the British, whose innate genius made global supremacy inevitable, that genius being inherent in the gene pool. This argument is nicely articulated by Thomas Williams in *Viking Britain,* William Collins, 2017, p42. I appreciate that this definition becomes somewhat blurred in other contexts where the concepts of racism and white supremacy are inextricably linked.
6. *Sunday Telegraph* 27th August 2017. *'Protesting against statues is just a way of showing off'*.

Part One

1. James Mallord William Turner RA (1775-1851). Amongst his relevant paintings are *The Slave Ship* (1840), *The Fighting Temeraire* (1838) and *The Battle of Trafalgar* (1822-4) as well as a number of sketches of HMS *Victory.*
2. Joseph Haydn wrote *'Missa in Angustiis'* in the summer of 1798. This subsequently became known as *'Nelsonmesse' (Nelson's Mass)*. Haydn performed the mass in the presence of Nelson in Eisenstadt in 1800. The story of their relationship can be found in *Admiral Nelson and Joseph Haydn'* Otto Erich Deutsch, The Nelson Society, 2000.

3. An excellent account of the Navy's first arctic voyage can be found in *Nelson's Arctic Voyage*, Peter Goodwin, Adlard Coles, 2018.
4. Thomas Paine, *Rights of Man* 1791. Paine was an English born, American political activist and a strong supporter of the French revolution which put him in direct conflict with conservative writers and thinkers of the day.
5. *The Guardian* 22nd August 2017, by the journalist Afua Hirsch.
6. For a summary of Nelson's appearances in the House of Lords see *Horatio Nelson,* Tom Pocock,The Bodley Head, 1987, pp 266-7.
7. William Huskisson who, incidentally, was an ardent abolitionist, quoted in John Sugden's *Nelson: The Sword of Albion*, The Bodley Head, 2012, p536.
8. For a full account of the events see *Nelson's Lost Jewel* Martyn Downer, The History Press, 2017, p76.
9. See Nelson's autobiography: *Nelson's Account of his Services* October 15th 1799, Port Mahon, reproduced in Robert Southey's *The Life of Nelson,* first published in 1813, with many subsequent reprints.
10. *Ibid.*
11. Nelson recalled the saying '*Aft the most honour: forward the better man*', common amongst the merchantmen. This implies that it was the ordinary seaman who carried the fight to the enemy whilst those officers, 'aft', received all the glory. This may well be explain why Nelson was determined to lead from the front as he did on the San Juan expedition and at the battles of St Vincent and Copenhagen.
12. See Christer Petley *Nelson and Slavery: Nelson's Dark Side' BBC History Magazine.* December 2018.
13. John Sugden *Nelson: A Dream of Glory* Pimlico 2005, p 162.
14. *Ibid*p258.
15. *Ibid* p259.
16. *Ibid* p259.
17. Nelson's enforcement of the Navigation Acts is covered in most biographies of Nelson and is covered in his own autobiography.

18. Letter to William Locker, 15th January 1785. See Victor Sharman *Nelson's Hero* Pen and Sword 1988.
19. Letter to Fanny, Nicolas, Vol. 1 p163.
20. Letter to Fanny 28th February 1787.
21. Patrick Delaforce *Nelson's First love: Fanny's Story,* Amberley Publishing, 1988, p29.
22. Christer Petley *'The Royal Navy, the British Atlantic Empire and the Abolition of the Slave Trade'* in *The Royal Navy and the British Atlantic World,* Palgrave MacMillan, 2016, Chapter 5.
23. *Ibid.*
24. *Ibid.*
25. Lt. Layman RN advocated replacement of slave labour with 'industrious' free, paid Chinese labour, a measure supported by Nelson.
26. See, for example, Stephen Tomkins *William Wilberforce: A Biography,* Lion Books, 2007, p 169.
27. See Nelson's autobiography, note 9 above.
28. N.A.M. Rodger *The Wooden World: An Anatomy of the Georgian Navy,* Fontana Press ,1986, pp 159-161.
29. *Ibid.*
30. Based on information provided by Professor Chris Waters, Heritage Department, National Park Authority, Nelson's Dockyard, Antigua.
31. Ray Costello *Black Salt: Seafarers of African Descent on British Ships* Liverpool University Press, 2012, e-version p 32.
32. See, for example, *The Black Heroes of Trafalgar,* article in *The Independent* 19th October 2005.
33. Letter to William Marsden at the Admiralty, 10th July 1805, penned aboard HMS *Victory,* Nicolas Vol. 6 pp.470-1.
34. *Ibid.*
35. Letter to William Marsden, Nicolas Vol. 7pp10-11.
36. Benjamin Silliman *A Journal of Travels in England, Holland and Scotland*1810.
37. Colin White *Nelson's Last Walk* The Nelson Society 2005.

38. 'Historycalroots' is a website aimed at, inter alia, 'raising awareness of the black and mixed heritage people who have played a part in shaping the way society looks today but whose role has been overlooked or not given the credit they are due'.
39. Thomas Pettigrew *Memoirs of the Life of Vice-Admiral Lord Viscount Nelson* Hardpress,2018 p 81.
40. Colin White *The New Nelson Letters* The Boydell Press, 2005, p 144.
41. Merton Place gardener, Thomas Cribb, quoted in Carola Oman, *Nelson,* Hodder and Stoughton, 1950, Chapter XV pp 435-65.
42. Julie Peakman *Emma Hamilton* Haus Publishing, 2005, p88.
43. See Thomas Blumel *Nelson's Overland Return in 1800,* The Nelson Society, 2000.
44. See for example Paul Youngquist (*Ed*), *Race, Romanticism and the Atlantic* Ashgate 2013, Chapter 8 *'Emma and Fatima Hamilton: Two Forms of Attitude'* by Elise Bruhl and Michael Garner.
45. *The Letters of Lord Nelson to Lady Hamilton,* London, 1814, Vol. 1p 92.
46. See Dr Nick Slope *Engage the Enemy More Closely*, 2010.
47. Nicolas Vol. 2 p131.
48. Nicolas Vol. 4 p125-6.
49. See footnote in Nicolas Vol. 4 p 119. Nelson had received a letter from Mr. Lucas, English Consul at Tripoli, on 14th October 1799.Nelson's sarcastic comment was written on the envelope.
50. Nicolas Vol. 4 p119.
51. For an introduction to the situation and geography of San Domingue see Sudhir Hazareesingh *The Black Spartacus: The Epic life of Toussaint Louverture* Penguin, 2021.
52. See Nicolas Vol. 6 p45.
53. A view recently expressed by George Blackshaw in his blog '*Nelson must Not Fall'* April 2021.
54. See, for example, Louis Morris '*Horatio Nelson: Turning a Blind Eye to Slavery*?' in *Uncomfortable Oxford* 5th August 2020.

Part Two

1. Sir Nicholas Harris Nicolas served in the Royal Navy between 1808 and 1816. After he retired at the end of the Napoleonic wars he turned to literary pursuits including publishing Nelson's correspondence.
2. Nelson letter to Captain Malcolm of HMS *Donegal* 11th June 1805, Nicolas Vol. 6 p457.
3. Nicolas *Ibid* Vol. 6 pp 452-5.
4. The information in this section on Simon Taylor is largely drawn from Christer Petley *White Fury: A Jamaican Slaveholder and the Age of Revolution*, a detailed examination of the life of Simon Taylor and his world.
5. See Christer Petley *'Nelson and Slavery: Nelson's Dark Side'* first published in *BBC History Magazine* Christmas 2018. Christer Petley is Professor of Atlantic History at the University of Southampton.
6. British library reference: Add MS 34959.
7. Dr Colin White describes Nelson as a *'wonderful wordsmith'* one *'whose sense is almost always clear'*. See *Nelson: The New Letters* Boydell Press, 2005.
8. Seymour Drescher *Econoside: British Slavery in the Era of Abolition*, Chapel Hill, University of North Carolina Press, 2nd Edition, 2010 p 19*.
9. NAM Rodger *The Command of the Ocean: A Naval History of Britain 1649-1815,* Penguin in association with the National Maritime Museum, 2004, pp 272-290*.
10. *As 8 and 9 above, quoted in University of Southampton Ph.D thesis by Sian Williams *'The Royal Navy in the Caribbean 1756-1815'* 2014.
11. See Nelson's Autobiography *Nelson's Account of His Services* October 15th 1799, Port Mahon.
12. Admiral John Byng was court-martialled for 'failing to do his utmost' to prevent Minorca falling to the French. Admiral Byng was found guilty and executed by firing squad on the quarter deck of HMS *Monarch* in March 1747. Whatever the merits of the case, a direct consequence of the sentence was to reinforce a naval officer's need to perform his duty to the utmost.

13. In summary *Habeas Corpus* is a recourse through law whereby a person can claim unlawful detention to a court and seek that the court determines whether or not the detention is lawful.
14. William Hazlitt (1778-1830) was an English social commentator, philosopher and literary critic. He was an ardent critic of, amongst others, the influential economist Malthus.
15. William Cobbett (1763-1835) was an English radical and an MP. He fought to abolish 'rotten boroughs', raise wages and ease poverty. He founded *'Cobbett's Weekly Political Register'* in 1802 which was a pre-cursor to Hansard.
16. For more details of the Haitian Revolution see Sudhir Hazareesingh *Black Spartacus: The Epic Life of Toussaint Louverture* Allen Lane, 2021.
17. Taylor to Nelson October 15th 1802. British Library, Egerton MS 1623 (Letters and Sonnets to Lord Nelson 1797-1805 f.34). Also reproduced in Thomas Pettigrew's *Memoirs of the life of Vice-Admiral Lord ViscountNelson',* 1849, p 588.
18. Nicolas *The Letters and Dispatches of Vice Admiral Lord Viscount Nelson* Vol. 6p413.
19. See Robert, Samuel and William Wilberforce *The Life of William Wilberforce* Cambridge University Press, 2011,Vol. 3 p 329.
20. Quoted in *White Fury, Ibid* end note 4, p 199.
21. Nicolas Vol. 6 p 455. Letter from Nelson to His Royal Highness The Duke of Clarence. It is well known that the Duke had pro-slavery leanings and he may well have passed this correspondence to the anti-abolitionists.
22. Angelina Gillian Osborne *Power and Persuasion: The London West India Committee, 1783-1833,* The University of Hull Ph.D thesis (available on-line at hydra.hull.ac.uk).
23. See also End Note 15 above.
24. A biography of the life of Rev Scott can be found in T.J.Pettigrew *The Memoirs of the Life of Vice-Admiral Lord Viscount Nelson* Vol. 2 pp 659-65.
25. See, for example, Michael Taylor *The Interest: How the British Establishment Resisted the Abolition of Slavery,* Vintage,2021.
26. Reported in *The Annual Register* (originally subtitled *A view of the History, Politicks and Literature of the Year)* which was founded in 1758, under the editorship of Edmund Burke.

27. See, for example, Christer Petley '*Lord Nelson and Slavery: Nelson's Dark Side'(Ibid)* which relies on the version in *Cobbett's Political Register* and *White Fury,* which appears to rely on the version in *The Naval Miscellany* although the quote is credited to the version in Nicolas Vol. 6 pp450-1 (see *White Fury* endnote 12 to Chapter 4).
28. Terry Colling *Close Examination Of Nelson's Correspondence* in *The Nelson Dispatch* Vol. 14 Part 5 Winter 2022 pp304-7.
29. *False Sanctity*, author unknown, Roake and Verity, London, 1831.
30. For a detailed assessment of the life of Lieutenant Layman see Dr.J.Sugden *The Stormy Life and Strange Death of Captain William Layman* in *The Trafalgar Chronicle*, no 22,2012) published by the 1805 Club.
31. Quoted in Stephen Tomkins *William Wilberforce: a Biography* Lion Books, 2007 p.155.
32. See John Marshall *Royal Naval Biography* Vol. 37 pp 440-68 (available on line).
33. *Ibid.*
34. *Ibid.*
35. See, for example, Ray Costello *Black Salt: Seafarers of African Descent on British Ships* Liverpool University Press, 2012.
36. See, for example, Martyn Downer *Nelson's Lost Jewel* p76 and Nicolas *The Dispatches and Letters of Vice Admiral Lord Viscount Nelson* Vol. 3 p231.
37. See Nicolas *The Dispatches and Letters of Vice Admiral Lord Viscount Nelson* Vol. 6 p412.
38. Dr Colin White points out in *Nelson: The New Letters* Boydell Press,2005 that " .... close examination of the British Library's volumes of pressed copy letters .... and comparison of their contents with those of Nelson's official letter-books kept by his secretaries, has shown that Nelson had recorded in them material that he regarded as **secret, or private**" (author's emphasis).
39. See, for example, *The Eastern Daily Press* 22 August 2020 *'Nelson Statue Vandalism Cost £2400 to Clean Up'.*

Part Three

1. See, for example, Jack Doyle '*Nelson Defiled'* in the *Daily Mail* April 17th 2018.
2. *The Nelson Dispatch* Vol. 14, Part 4, Autumn 2021 p197. Extract from a speech by Martyn Downer given to The Nelson Society on 23rd October 2021.
3. *The Slave Trade and the British Empire: An Audit of Commemoration in Wales* Task Force and Finish Group Report and Audit, 26 November 2020.
4. Alice Procter *The Whole Picture* Cassell, 2020.
5. *Ibid* Chapter 19, 'The Ship'.
6. (Procter gives the reference in an end note as Nicolas Vol. VI. p 45. This should read p 450).
7. Zewditu Gebreyohanes *Protecting Local Heritage; How to bring democracy to the renaming of local streets* The Policy Exchange, 2021.
8. Stephen Mullen *'Glasgow, Slavery and Atlantic Commerce: An Audit of Historic Connections and Modern Legacies'* March 2022.
9. Matthew Sheldon '*Nelson on a Pedestal'* www.nmrn.org.uk/news-events/nelson-pedestal 18th June 2020.
10. Craig Simpson '*Legacy Review Could Knock Nelson off his Pedestal'* ,*The Sunday Telegraph* 11th October 2020.
11. (Akala) *Natives; Race and Class in the Ruins of Empire,* Two Roads, 2018.
12. *Ibid* p145.

SELECT BIBLIOGRAPHY AND NOTE ON SOURCES

As I noted in the Foreword to this study, I did not intend to cover the well-documented life of Nelson (which obviously provides part of the 'context' to this study). To examine this further I would recommend:

Admiral Lord Nelson *Nelson's Account of his Services* (reproduced in Southey's Life of Nelson1813).
Clarke and McArthur *The Life and Services of Horatio Viscount Nelson* Fisher Son &Co 1839-40.
C.Hibbert *Nelson: A Personal History* Penguin Books Ltd 1994.
A.Lambert *Nelson: Britannia's God of War* Faber and Faber Ltd 2004.
Capt. A.T. Mahan *The Life of Nelson* Sampson Low, Marston & Co. 1899.
C. Oman *Nelson* Hodder and Stoughton 1950.
T. Pocock *Horatio Nelson* The Bodley Head 1987.
R.Southey *The Life of Nelson* (originally published in 1813).
J. Sugden *A Dream of Glory* (biography Vol. 1) Pimlico 2005.
J.Sugden *The Sword of Albion* (biography Vol. 2) The Bodley Head 2012.

To assist in understanding the Navy and the Caribbean of the period, I found the following particularly useful:

R. Costello *Black Salt: Seafarers of African Descent on British Ships* Liverpool University Press 2012.
M. Duffy *Soldiers, Sugar and Seapower* Oxford University Press 1987.
S. Hazareesingh *Black Spartacus: the Epic Life of Toussaint Louverture* Penguin 2021.
D.Howarth *British Sea Power* Robinson 2003.
V.K. Hubbard *Swords, Ships and Sugar: A History of Nevis* Premier Editions International, Inc 2002.
B.Lavery *Empire of the Seas* Conway 2012.

D.V. Nicholson *English Harbour: The First 2000 Years* Scrip.J, Trinidad and Tobago 2002.
C. Petley *White Fury* Oxford University Press 2018.
C. Petley *'The Royal Navy and the British Atlantic World, c1750-1820'* Chapter 5Palgrave MacMillan 2016.
N.A.M. Rodger *The Command of the Ocean: A Naval History of Britain 1649-1815* Fontana Press 1988.
M.Taylor *The Interest* Vintage Digital 2020.

Other relevant books are (but not exclusively) :

Akala *Natives:Race and Class in the Ruins of Empire* Two Roads 2018.
M. Downer *Nelson's Lost Jewel* The History Press 2017.
P.Delaforce *Nelson's First Love: Fanny's Story* Amberley Publishing 1988.
R.J. Evans *In Defence of History* Granta Books 2018.
A.Forrest *Napoleon* Quercus 2011.
P.Goodwin *Nelson's Arctic Voyage* Adlard Coles 2018.
W. Hague *William Wilberforce* Harper Perennial 2008
A.Hirsch *Brit(ish):On Race, Identity and Belonging* Jonathan Cape 2018.
R. Knight *William IV: A King at Sea* Penguin Books, Penguin Monarchs Series, 2015.
J.Marshall *Royal Naval Biography* Cambridge University Press 2010.
A.Procter *The Whole Picture* Cassell 2020.
T. Pettigrew *Memoirs of the Life of Vice-Admiral Lord Viscount Nelson'* Hardpress 2018, originally published 1849.
T. Pocock *The Sailor King: The Life of King William IV* Lume Books 2020.
S.Sanghera *Empireland: How Imperialism Has Shaped Modern Britain* Penguin 2021.
V.Sharman *Nelson's Hero* Pen and Sword 2005.
D. Snow *Death or Victory* Harper Press 2009
S.Tomkins *William Wilberforce: A Biography* Lion Books 2007.

R, S, and W Wilberforce *The Life of William Wilberforce* (3 Volumes) Cambridge University Press 2011.
Walton Look Lai *The Chinese in the West Indies 1808-1950: A Documentary History* academia.edu (website) 1997

Nelson's published letters are an important source of information. However, as pointed out at the beginning of Part Two of this study, they have their limitations and need to be approached with a degree of caution. In addition to the published volumes, numerous hitherto unpublished letters have come to light, primarily in the hands of private collectors. The 're-discovery' of the Bridport collection in the British Library, and an analysis of the collection in 2005 by Dr Colin White, shed new light on our understanding as to how Nelson's published letters have been manipulated, altered and edited, for a range of motives. The lesson is clear: original letters should be used, wherever possible, to assist in forming judgements about Nelson, as in the case of the Nelson-Taylor letter of June 1805. (The irony of my using published versions of Nelson letters, particularly those in Nicolas, in support of my analysis, is not lost on me!). The following are particularly relevant:

Sir N.H.Nicolas *'The Letters and Dispatches of Vice Admiral Lord Viscount Nelson'* (6 Volumes) Chatham Publishing 1998, first published 1844-46.
C.White *Nelson:The New Letters* Boydell Press 2005.
M.Czisnik *Admiral Nelson: Image and Icon* Edinburgh University Ph.D thesis Vol. 2, 2002.

The letters of King William IV were deposited in the Royal Archives in 1912. William had ordered his papers destroyed by Sir Henry Wheatley, Keeper of his Privy Purse, but that order was not fully carried out. The saved correspondence seems to be of little relevance to this study.
An important resource is the UCL *'Legacies of British Slave Ownership'* which records those who benefitted from the compensation scheme after the abolition of the slave trade.

In the text I have referred to Cobbett's *Political Register* and the *Annual Register.* These can be accessed on-line. I have also referred to numerous articles, details of which can be found in the Endnotes. I would draw particular attention to Christer Petley's article, published in the BBC History Magazine, entitled '*Nelson's Dark Side'.* Terry Colling's article, published in *The Nelson Dispatch* (which is the journal of The Nelson Society), entitled '*Close Examination of Nelson's Correspondence',* was also most illuminating.
I found several Ph.D theses of particular help. These are referenced in the End Notes, especially those by Sian Williams (End Notes 8, 9 and 10, Part Two) and Angelina Osborne (End Note 22, Part Two).

Finally *The Nelson Dispatch,* which has been published quarterly since 1982, is a particularly useful source of information on all things Nelson. All copies are available online to Nelson Society members.

ACKNOWLEDGEMENTS

I have always wanted to write a book about Nelson but I never imagined it would be on the subject of Nelson and the slave trade. I was asked to write an article, for publication in *The Nelson Dispatch*, investigating the allegations that Nelson was a racist and white supremacist. Those investigations led to the discovery of the forged copy of Nelson's letter to the wealthy plantation owner Simon Taylor, which was used after Nelson's death to try to influence the outcome of debates in Parliament on the Abolition of the Slave Trade Act. My article was published in the Autumn of 2020.

My research at that time was supported by Martyn Downer, a world leader and renowned author in respect of relics and artefacts relating to life and times of Admiral Lord Nelson, who kindly furnished a copy of the forged letter from Nelson to Simon Taylor. I owe much to Martyn's invaluable comments and input on the text of this book.

Valuable comments on the historical accuracy of the text were offered by the Nelson Society historian, Ray Aldis, to whom I am deeply indebted. Any errors are, of course, mine. Thanks must go to Peregrine Nelson Hood, President of the Nelson Society, whose enthusiasm for all things Nelson shone through his encouragement to write this book.

Especial thanks go to Dr John Sugden, arguably Nelson's foremost biographer, for his comments on the text and providing the Preface to this book.

I am particularly grateful to Susan Morris, Executive Editor of *The Nelson Dispatch,* for her careful readings of the manuscript and constructive comments on style, and to Peter Clayton who brought his considerable skills and knowledge of publishing to bear in readying the book for publication.

Last but not least my love and thanks to my long-suffering wife, Beryl, who has not only supported me in this venture but read the first complete draft of the book, and has had to put up with that third person in our marriage, Admiral Lord Nelson.

INDEX

Page numbers in *italics* refer to illustrations.

abolitionists 27, 52 *see also* Wilberforce, William
Act for the Abolition of the Slave Trade 1807 95, 117
Akala: *Natives: Race and Class in the Ruins of Empire* 121
anti-abolitionists 18, 37
  alterations to Nelson–Taylor letter 78–84, 87, 88–90, 108–9
  False Sanctity booklet 96–100, *97*
  planter society 28, 30–33, 62–64, 146–47
Antigua 29–31, *31,32,* 38–40, 83

Barbary slave trade 54–56, 106
BBC History Magazine 16, 64
Black Lives Matter movement 17
black sailors 38–42, *39,40see also* Marguette, James
Bonne Citoyenne, HMS 25
British Library, Bridport Papers 64–68

Campbell, Duncan 86–87
Campbell version of the Nelson–Taylor letter 85–90, *86,136–137,* 138–39
Canning, George 101–2
Caribbean islands (West Indies) *34*
  Nelson and (*see* Nelson, Admiral Lord (Horatio), West Indies visits)
  role in British empire 36–37, 51–52, 53, 67–70
  see also Antigua; Dominica; Jamaica; Nevis; Saint-Domingue; Trinidad
Castillo (black sailor) 38
Castle Museum, Norwich 117–18
Chinese labourers 102–4, 106
Chretien, General Joseph 75–76, 106
Christian, Admiral 53
Clarence, Duke of *see* William Henry, Prince
Clarke, J. S. and J. McArthur: *The Life and Services of Horatio Viscount Nelson* 61, 93, 94, 140
Cobbett, William *65,* 73
  Political Register 64, 77, 83–84, 92, 95, *135*
Collingwood, Cuthbert 30
Collingwood, William 30
colonial system 36–37, 51–52, 67–70
compensation for slave owners 113
Cornwallis, Cuba 28, 29, 47–48
Cornwallis, William 47
Costello, Ray 40

Davison, Alexander 62, 82–83
Despard, Catherine 49–50
Despard, Edward 49

Dighton, Denis: *The Death of Nelson* 38, *40*
Dominica 52–53
Downer, Martyn 64
Duckworth, Sir John 56–57
Dundas, Henry 36

Efendi, Kelim 25
Ellis, J. D. 45–46
Equiano, Olaudah 40–41, *41*

False Sanctity (anonymous) 96–100, *97*

Gardner, Desley 38–40
George III, King 51, 52
Georgian era context 21–22
Glasgow City Council audit: *Glasgow, Slavery and Atlantic Commerce* 118
Goldsmiths, University of London, consultation on statues 114
Grenville, William, 1st Baron Grenville 95
Guardian newspaper article 16, 22–23, 34, 58–59

Haiti *see* Saint-Domingue
Hamilton, Lady Emma 25–26, 46, 48–49
Hamilton, Fatima 48–49
Hamilton, Sir William 73
Hazlitt, William 73
Herbert, John (Fanny Nelson's uncle) 32, 51–52, *151,* 154
Hirsch, Afua *see Guardian* newspaper article
Historic England 111–12
Hochschild, Adam 100
Hood, (later Sir) Samuel (1762–1814) 102–3
Hood, Samuel, 1st Viscount Hood (1724–1816) 29, 85
House of Commons 27, 51, 52, 53, 71–72
House of Lords 23–24, 51–52, 80, 95

Jamaica
  Nelson and 27–28, 29, 47–48
  Nelson–Taylor letter references 78–79, 82–83
  Prince William Henry (Duke of Clarence) and 80–81, 82, 85
  Simon Taylor and 62–64

Kelly, Guy 115

Laughton, John Knox: *Naval Miscellany* 93, 94, 107, 108, 142–43
Layman, Lieutenant William 101–4, *105,* 106
Locker, William 27, 29, 30–31, 52–53
London West India Committee 63, 81

Marguette, James 43–46
Marsden, William 44–45, 62, 75, 80

Mary Ann (merchantman) 26–27, 37, 40
Middle Ground settlement, Antigua 38–40

National Maritime Museum, Greenwich 120
National Museum of the Royal Navy, Portsmouth 119–20 *see also* Nelson–Taylor letter, NMRN version
Native Americans 28
Naval Miscellany (Laughton) 93, 94, 107, 108, 142–43
Navigation Acts 30, 40, 70, 76
Nelson, Revd Edmund (Nelson's father) 48
Nelson, Frances (Fanny) (formerly Nisbet, née Woolward) 31–33, 48, 85
Nelson, Admiral Lord (Horatio) *4, 40*
accusations against 22–23, 109
black acquaintances
Cuba Cornwallis 28, 29, 47–48
Catherine Despard 49–50
Fatima Hamilton 48–49
James Marguette 43–46
James Price 46–47
Hercules Ross 27
chronology of his life 13–15
and the Duke of Clarence 85
his handwriting 148–50, *149*
his humane and pragmatic approach 106–7
his 'influence' 24–26
his paternalism 73–74
his sense of duty 69–70
House of Lords speeches 23–24
and William Layman 101–4, 106
letters referencing race or slavery 33–34, 51–57, 108
re Barbary slave trade 54–56
to Sir John Duckworth re Saint-Domingue 56–57
to John Herbert 51–52, *151,* 154
to William Locker 52–53
pressed copies 64–68
printed sources 61
see also Nelson–Taylor letter
and Native Americans 28
secures freedom of slaves 24–25, 106
statues and memorials 16–17, 38, 109, 111–12, 114, 117, 126
West Indies visits 118
1771–72, aged thirteen on a merchantman 26–27, 37, 40
1777–80, Jamaica 27–28
1782–83, captain of the *Albemarle* 28–29, 85
1784–87, Antigua 29–33, 85
1805, in pursuit of the French 33–35, *34,* 43–44, 61–62
Nelson Ward, Norwich 116–17
Nelson's Column, Great Yarmouth 117
Nelson's Column, Trafalgar Square 16–17, 38, 111–12, 115, 121
Nelson–Taylor letter 16, 62, 108–9
Campbell version 85–90, *86, 136–137,* 138–39

Cobbett's *Political Register* version 64, 77, 83–84, 92, 95, *135*
False Sanctity version 96–100, *97*
key phrases
the 'Good old school' 68–70
'in a thousand fears' for Jamaica 78–79
'just rights' 70, 79
the 'Public' 84
the sign off 79–80
summary table 93–94
Wilberforce and his 'damnable cruel doctrine' 74–77, 79
Wilberforce and his 'hypocritical allies' 72–74
Laughton's *Naval Miscellany* version 93, 94, 107, 108, 142–43
NMRN version 64, 78–83, 87, 88, *131,* 133–34, 148–50
Popham, used in defence of 90–92
post-script addition 80–83
pressed copy of the original 66–68, *127–130*
timeline of its use 144–45
unattributed reference in Hochschild 100
Nevis 31, 32
newspaper articles 16, 22–23, 34, 58–59, 115, 119, 120
Nicaragua (San Juan expedition) 28, 47, 49
Nicolas, Sir Nicholas Harris: *The Dispatches and Letters of Vice Admiral Lord Viscount Nelson* 61, 93, 141
Nisbet, Fanny *see* Nelson, Frances (Fanny)
Nisbet, Josiah 32
Norfolk Naval Pillar, Great Yarmouth 117
Norwich, effects of denigrating Nelson's reputation 109, 116–18

Palermo, Sicily 24–25, 106
parliamentary inquiry into the slave trade, 1790 27, 36, 37, 71, 119
Petley, Christer 16, 28, 64, 113
Pitt, William, the Younger 36–37, 104
planters 18, 28, 30–33, 62–64, 146–47 *see also* Taylor, Simon
Political Register (Cobbett) 64, 77, 83–84, 92, 95, *135*
Popham, Sir Home Riggs 90–92, *92*
Pratt, Sir John Jeffreys 88, *89*
Price, James 46–47
pro-slavery lobby *see* anti-abolitionists
Procter, Alice 115–16

Rathbone, John 26–27
Ross, Hercules 27
Royal Navy, role and attitudes of 36–42, 69–70, 76, 108, 119–20

Saint-Domingue (St/San Domingo) 56–57, 74–76
San Juan expedition (Nicaragua) 28, 47, 49
Scott, Reverend Dr Alexander 62, 84
Scott, John (Nelson's secretary) 84, 88, 148–50
Sheldon, Matthew 119–20
Silliman, Benjamin 45
slave owners, compensation for 113

Slave Trade Act 1807 95, 117
slaves
  Barbary slave trade 54–56, 106
  employed on ships as free men 24–25, 38–42, 106
  female, as mistresses 27
  release of Turkish 24–25, 106
  Saint-Domingue revolution 56–57, 74–76
  status in the Navigation Acts 76
St Domingo *see* Saint-Domingue
St Paul's Cathedral website 119
statues
  erection of new 126
  removal or vandalism 16–17, 109, 111–12, 114, 115
  symbolism of Nelson's Column 121
Suckling, Captain Maurice (Nelson's uncle) 26, 27, 46–47
Suckling, William (Nelson's uncle) 32, 46
Sugden, John 30, 64
Sunday Telegraph newspaper article 120

Taylor, Michael 99–100
Taylor, Simon (slave-owning planter) 28, 62–64, 75, 79–80, 81, 146–47 *see also* Nelson–Taylor letter
Telegraph newspaper articles 115, 119
Trinidad 101–4
Triumph, HMS 26–27
Turkish slaves, release of 24–25, 106

UCL (University College London) website 'Legacies of British Slave Ownership' 113

Vansittart, Nicholas 103–4
Victory, HMS *40,* 41–42, 44, 61–62, 84, 121
Villeneuve, Admiral 33, 43, 79

Waters, Christopher 38–40
Welsh Assembly audit: *The Slave Trade and the British Empire* 112–13
West Indies *see* Caribbean islands
White, Colin 45, 65–66, 107–8
Wilberforce, William 36–37, 53, 70–77, *72,* 98, 102, 104, 108
William Henry, Prince (later Duke of Clarence, then King William IV) 29, 31, 47, 62, 74, 80–83, *82,* 85
Woolward, William 32
Wyndham, William 54, 55–56

Index prepared by Wendy Baskett, Pinpoint Indexing

THE NELSON SOCIETY

The Nelson Society is a registered charity, with a worldwide membership, whose object is to advance public education and awareness of the life and times and achievements of Admiral Lord Nelson and his navy.

The object of the Society is furthered through the publication of a quarterly journal *The Nelson Dispatch,* events, lectures and an active social calendar. The Society supports appropriate good causes relevant to Nelson and his world with grants, advice, consultancy, and supports conservation projects. The Society encourages and undertakes research and publishes original material both through the *Dispatch* and as stand-alone publications.

The Society has no headquarters but is managed by a committee of volunteers elected by the membership. The Nelson Society can be followed on its Facebook page,**The Nelson Society UK** ,and more information is available on the Society's website **www.nelson-society.com**.

Printed in Great Britain
by Amazon

34991429R00099